DIFFERENTIATED READING INSTRUCTION

Differentiated Reading Instruction

STRATEGIES FOR THE PRIMARY GRADES

Sharon Walpole
Michael C. McKenna

THE GUILFORD PRESS
New York   London

©2007 The Guilford Press
A Division of Guilford Publications, Inc.
72 Spring Street, New York, NY 10012
www.guilford.com

Printed in the United States of America

This book is printed on acid-free paper.

Last digit is print number: 9 8 7 6 5 4 3

Library of Congress Cataloging-in-Publication Data
Walpole, Sharon.
    Differentiated reading instruction : strategies for the primary grades /
Sharon Walpole, Michael C. McKenna.
        p. cm.
    Includes bibliographical references and index.
    ISBN-13: 978-1-59385-412-6 (pbk. : alk. paper)
    ISBN-10: 1-59385-412-9 (pbk. : alk. paper)
    ISBN-13: 978-1-59385-413-3 (hardcover : alk. paper)
    ISBN-10: 1-59385-413-7 (hardcover : alk. paper)
    1. Reading (Primary) 2. Individualized reading instruction. I. McKenna,
Michael C. II. Title.
    LB1525.56.W35 2007
    372.4—dc22
                                                            2006037386

*To the literacy coaches and teachers in Georgia
who have given us the opportunity and the charge
to be more specific about differentiation*

About the Authors

Sharon Walpole, PhD, is Assistant Professor in the School of Education at the University of Delaware. She has extensive school-based experience, including both high school teaching and elementary school administration. Dr. Walpole served as a research assistant and as a research associate at the Center for the Improvement of Early Reading Achievement. She has also been involved in federally funded and homegrown schoolwide reform projects and participates in and studies the design and effects of schoolwide reforms, particularly those involving literacy coaches. She is the coauthor (with Michael C. McKenna) of *The Literacy Coach's Handbook: A Guide to Research-Based Practice* and has written articles in the *Journal of Educational Psychology*; *Reading and Writing Quarterly*; the *Journal of Speech, Language, and Hearing Services in Schools*; *Early Education and Development*; and *The Reading Teacher*. Dr. Walpole's research interests include classroom- and school-level correlates of student achievement, particularly in schools engaged in improvement efforts.

Michael C. McKenna, PhD, is Thomas G. Jewell Professor of Reading at the University of Virginia. He is the author, coauthor, or editor of 15 books and more than 100 articles, chapters, and technical reports on a range of literacy topics. His books include *The Literacy Coach's Handbook* (with Sharon Walpole), *Assessment for Reading Instruction, Help for Struggling Readers, Teaching through Text,* and *Issues and Trends in Literacy Education,* among others. Dr. McKenna's research has been sponsored by the National Reading Research Center and the Center for the Improvement of Early Reading Achievement. He is the cowinner of the National Reading Conference's Edward Fry Book Award and the American Library Association's Award for Outstanding Academic Books. He serves on the editorial board of *Reading Research Quarterly,* and his articles have appeared in that journal as well as in the *Journal of Educational Psychology, Educational Researcher, The Reading Teacher,* and others. He has coedited themed issues of the *Peabody Journal of Education* and *Reading and Writing Quarterly.* Dr. McKenna's research interests include comprehension in content settings, reading attitudes, technology applications, and beginning reading.

Preface

We have spent the last several years working with teachers, reading specialists, literacy coaches, principals, and district representatives committed to the concept of leaving no children behind in elementary school literacy instruction. That work—as you can well imagine—has been challenging and rewarding; we have partnered with some wonderful educators. That work has also engaged us in a series of trial-by-fire experiments; we have worked hard to introduce new concepts in ways that result in maximum gain for children and maximum flexibility for schools. In this book, we share lessons that will support gains in student achievement and also provide teachers with choices. The lessons that we have chosen are those that we have shared with teachers who are asking the most important question that we can imagine, and also the one that we are most frequently asked: How can we meet children's diverse needs and accelerate literacy development for all within regular classroom instruction?

The short answer is this: We can do much better by applying what we already know about effective instruction. We can design a daily literacy block that is sensible and sensitive, one that leaves neither teachers nor children behind. We will show you what we have learned about that design, and we will try to provide you with a conceptual map as you make your own plans for your own students. Throughout the book, you will hear us urge you to be planful and flexible. Both are important if we are to meet the needs of more and more children each day and each year.

There are two principal audiences for this book. First, if you are working in a schoolwide reading reform initiative, such as a Comprehensive School Reform project, a Title I school improvement project, a Reading First initiative, or a school- or district-level literacy reform, this book will help you to provide some structure and direction to the time that you have protected for small-group instruction. We have worked in many schools with such programs, and they typically share a common approach—they bring about achievement gains through restructuring their professional support system, reconsidering their whole-group instruction, and reexamining how they use their materials. Once those gains are realized, though, they know that they must direct their resources toward meeting children's individual needs in order to continue to improve achievement. That change is much more difficult to accomplish. This book is structured so that the ideas it contains can be used within any larger curriculum reform, as long as they are nested carefully inside the time that is protected for meeting children's individual needs.

Another audience for this book is the many inquiring teachers who are simply considering their own classroom-based instruction. Some of those teachers have access to very rich curriculum resources; others do not. We have teachers in both sets of circumstances in mind, and we hope that all will find some of the ideas we are sharing both realistic and targeted. One thing that is as true today as it has ever been is that instruction is effective only to the extent that it moves children forward in skills and strategies from wherever they begin; that means that we will never be able to serve children in schools by projecting a one-size-fits-all model.

You may want to use this book in pieces according to your own interests or the current needs of your students. We invite you to do that. However, we hope that you will consider reading the first two chapters, the general model and assessment chapters, before you begin. It will be difficult for you to envision the use of the instructional ideas that come later unless you have understood how and why you might schedule your literacy instructional block and how and why you might use data to group students for instruction and to determine their instructional needs.

As this is a book about responding to the diverse needs of children, we provide a glossary that anticipates the diverse needs of our own audience. Some terms we have been careful to define in context, but if you encounter a word we do not define and with which you are not already familiar, the chances are good that you will find it in the glossary. We doubt that any of the terms will be truly new, but we anticipate that we may sometimes use new labels for concepts of which you have at least partial understanding.

Contents

CHAPTER 1

Planning
Differentiated Instruction

What *is* differentiated instruction anyway? The answer is that it depends upon whom you ask! As with the terms "balanced reading" or "balanced instruction," we may be losing focus by being too inclusive. The terms "small-group instruction," "flexibly grouped instruction," "differentiated instruction," and "needs-based instruction" each may mean very specific things to certain people, but those meanings may be very different. We want to be clear from the start that we do have a specific meaning in mind when we think about differentiated instruction.

One very popular model of differentiated instruction is Carol Ann Tomlinson's, which we first learned about through a great book: *The Differentiated Classroom: Responding to the Needs of All Learners* (1999). In that book, Tomlinson presents models for teachers to use to design units with differentiated outcomes; students participate in some instruction and activities together, and then they choose (or are assigned) different projects and opportunities to demonstrate what they have learned—and those demonstrations vary in complexity. This is a fantastic model for the design of social studies or science instruction in response to new state standards; in fact, one of us (S.W.) participated in elementary school curriculum design using this model with the help of a gifted education specialist. That, however, is not the type of differentiation we mean.

Another very popular model for differentiation is that found in Irene Fountas and Gay-Su Pinnell's (1996) work, *Guided Reading: Good First Teaching for All Children*. In that model, teachers use oral reading to assess children's instructional reading level—that level of text at which they can read with 95–97% accuracy—

1

and then provide them with guided opportunities to read and reread texts at that level, reflecting on their oral reading successes and errors and then moving them through a set of leveled texts. That is not the type of differentiation we mean either, as all children get the same type of fluency and comprehension instruction with different texts.

So what do we mean? First of all, we believe that all children (even children whose achievement is well ahead of grade level) deserve classroom-based literacy instruction that helps them accomplish challenging tasks that are just out of their reach. Second, we mean instruction that targets a particular group of children's needs directly and temporarily—differentiated instruction is both driven and monitored by assessment. Third, we mean instruction that applies a developmental model and assumes that children might have needs in word recognition, in fluency, in oral vocabulary, and in comprehension, but that in order to reach higher-level reading comprehension goals, we first must help children achieve automatic access to words. And, finally, we mean instruction that supplements high-quality, grade-level, whole-group instruction.

INSTRUCTIONAL TIERS

Reading First, that portion of the No Child Left Behind Act of 2002 that provides funding for kindergarten-through-third-grade schoolwide reforms, while not without its critics, has provided a fast-forwarded national dialogue about the design of effective reading programs. It would be foolish not to consider those ideas as potentially useful in other sites. Among the most important ideas advanced by Reading First is that of tiered instruction. Figure 1.1 presents a visual model for the concept of tiered instruction. The idea is this: The basic foundation of curriculum and instruction in any classroom at any grade level is the instruction that is provided for all—whole-group instruction. That instruction must be conceptually rich

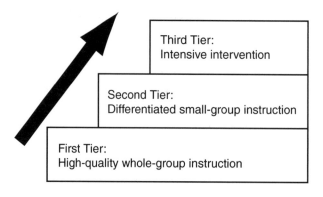

FIGURE 1.1. Three tiers of instruction.

and challenging; it must build knowledge, skills, and strategies; it must be linked to state and national standards for excellence; it must be informed by research; and it must be crafted and recrafted each day by reflective teachers. Not all of that instruction will be teacher directed, of course. By whole group, we mean here that all children in the classroom participate in the same set of activities. The activities will likely include direct instruction from the teacher, group work, individual practice, and assessments. One measure of the success of such a curricular plan is the percentage of children who achieve one year's growth in one year's time (and we realize that quantifying such growth is problematic). However, think of it this way—high-quality whole-group instruction plus some small-group support should be adequate to support almost all children who begin the year with grade-level achievement in accomplishing what they need to move to the next grade right on target.

Tier 2 instruction represents a more complex and targeted (and probably shorter) portion of the instructional day. This is time set aside for differentiated instruction; children are working in small groups, formed and reformed by the teacher, and one group is working directly with the teacher while the others are engaged in meaningful literacy practice. We favor curriculum plans where *all* children—not just those who are struggling—participate in Tier 2. That is the time for accelerated and challenging work for the children who are achieving above grade level, for extra attention to current lessons for those who are at or near grade level, and for reteaching of previous skills and strategies for children who are struggling. These are the target children for the second tier, and we expect that as many as one-half of them will experience enough growth that they finish the year with at least grade-level achievement.

For children for whom both Tier 1 and Tier 2 are insufficient, this organizational plan includes a safety net. Tier 3 instruction is even more targeted. In fact, it often includes a carefully designed curriculum that is meant to provide especially systematic and explicit instruction. In the past, Tier 3 instruction was reserved for those children qualifying for special education services. Currently, though, many districts are much more flexible in their programs and allow all children to participate in the instruction that they need as soon as their teachers know that they need it. This approach—more responsive and more temporary—is aimed at preventing children from needing special education services by providing more flexible regular education options.

As we move up the steps from Tier 1 to Tier 2 to Tier 3, we focus more specifically and directly on children's needs. There is mounting evidence that such a differentiation plan is practical for teachers and schools and will allow for literacy acceleration for children. William Bursuck and his colleagues (Bursuck et al., 2004) described Project PRIDE, a schoolwide reform implemented in three high-poverty, ethnically diverse schools. The project used a three-tier instructional approach. Tier 1, basic instruction, was provided for all children by classroom teachers using their core instructional materials (a set of basal readers). The teachers in the project worked together to understand how to use those materials in ways that maximized student engagement.

Tier 2, differentiated instruction, was delivered by classroom teachers and by others (paraprofessionals, specialists) to needs-based groups of two to eight students whose progress in specific areas was insufficient. Tier 2 consisted of review and practice of essential skills from the core scope and sequence. In kindergarten, Tier 2 lasted for 10 minutes each day. In first and second grade, it lasted for 30 minutes. For students whose literacy achievement was not accelerated with the combination of Tiers 1 and 2, Tier 3 instruction took place outside the classroom with a separate, highly specialized curriculum. Daily sessions lasted from 30 to 50 minutes with group sizes of two to five. Compared with a control school with similar demographics but not organizing instruction in this way, this instructional model was effective in increasing the percentage of children who met achievement benchmarks by the end of the year and in reducing the number of at-risk children. This is one example of how effective a three-tier approach can be in meeting the needs of all learners.

INSTRUCTIONAL DIETS AND GROUPINGS

The concept of tiered instruction, while conceptually elegant, does little to help an individual teacher know what to teach when. In fact, anyone who would call instructional planning simple has neither spent much time in a classroom nor ever unpacked a set of core program materials! Teachers have (and make) many choices in the course of instructional planning. Some are made in advance, and some are made during the course of instruction. We think the best classrooms have an underlying instructional structure that guides both sets of plans—the ones made before and during instruction. In *The Literacy Coach's Handbook: A Guide to Research-Based Instruction* (Walpole & McKenna, 2004), we shared the concept of an instructional diet. An instructional diet, like any diet, is a set of guidelines that help an individual meet his or her health goals. Generally, diets specify how much and what kinds of foods to eat.

Figure 1.2 is the instructional diet that we have been using in our work with literacy coaches. The "food groups" in the diet are phonemic awareness, decoding, fluency, vocabulary, comprehension, and writing. You will see that at different ages, we anticipate that children need different amounts of time and emphasis on specific components of literacy development.

Figure 1.3 takes those same components and presents them in a different way. Again, looking across the grade levels, there are shifts in attention. But this time, we emphasize the fact that some components of the curriculum are probably

	Phonemic awareness	Decoding	Fluency	Vocabulary	Comprehension strategies	Writing
K	20%	10%	20%	30%	10%	10%
1	10%	20%	20%	20%	10%	20%
2		10%	30%	10%	30%	20%
3			20%	20%	30%	30%

FIGURE 1.2. A model for instructional time by grade level. From Walpole and McKenna (2004). Copyright 2004 by The Guilford Press. Reprinted by permission.

better addressed in small groups. Luckily, others are actually better addressed in large groups. We want you to keep these estimates in mind as you use this text; while we will be focusing much of our attention on phonemic awareness and phonics for kindergarten and first grade, that is because we are targeting only that small-group, needs-based, differentiated time in your instructional diet. If you did not provide the rest of the instruction (e.g., the vocabulary and comprehension development that comes as essential fare in early primary read-alouds), you would have an unbalanced diet indeed. That is not our goal. We want to support you in making better use of that small-group time, but we also want you to continue with best practices in your whole-group plan.

	Phonemic awareness	Decoding	Fluency	Vocabulary	Comprehension strategies
K	Needs-based group	Whole group and needs-based group	Whole group and needs-based group	Whole group	Whole group
1	Needs-based group	Whole group and needs-based group	Whole group and needs-based group	Whole group	Whole group
2	Intervention only	Needs-based group	Whole group and needs-based group	Whole group	Whole group and needs-based group
3		Intervention only	Whole group and needs-based group	Whole group and needs-based group	Whole group and needs-based group

FIGURE 1.3. A model for grouping time by grade level and component. From Walpole and McKenna (2004). Copyright 2004 by The Guilford Press. Reprinted by permission.

DIFFERENTIATION AND FAIRNESS

One barrier to teachers' implementing truly differentiated instruction is their lingering fear that it is somehow "unfair" to give children different types and amounts of instruction. Research says that it is fair, as long as you define "fair" as providing an individual child opportunities for maximum growth. Connor, Morrison, and Katch (2004) have addressed that issue recently. These researchers linked teachers' instructional practices to growth in student achievement. They observed first-grade instruction in 42 classrooms and measured achievement for 108 target children. In their observations, they described instruction as either explicit (when children's attention is directly focused on strategies) or implicit (when skills might be developed more incidentally). They also coded instruction as either teacher managed (with the teacher responsible for directing each child's learning) or child managed (with the child responsible for directing his or her own learning, as in independent work). They measured change in these dimensions, to investigate whether teachers adapted their routines over the course of the year as children's skills changed.

Findings indicated that students achieved more growth when their instruction was matched to their needs—different children with different needs benefited from different opportunities. Children who began the first-grade year with weak decoding skills and low vocabulary skills had more growth in decoding in classrooms with more time in teacher-managed explicit instruction and less time in child-managed implicit practice. In contrast, for children who began the first-grade year with strong decoding and vocabulary skills, the amount of time teachers spent in teacher-managed explicit instruction was not important. Instead, it was the amount of child-managed implicit instruction—reading and writing practice—that produced the highest growth pattern. For children who began the first-grade year with high vocabulary and low decoding scores, more time in teacher-managed explicit instruction led to more growth in decoding.

These findings are related to the development of a sound differentiation plan that serves the needs of *all* children. The study indicates that providing all children the same amount of teacher-managed explicit instruction is not the best way to promote growth in decoding. Rather, children whose initial achievement scores indicate that they have significant needs in vocabulary and decoding benefit from more time in direct instruction while children with the opposite profile (strong vocabulary, strong decoding) actually grow more if they spend more time in reading and writing practice. In most classrooms, the realities of scheduling and managing children require that in order for the teacher to provide additional small-group differentiated instructional time to one group of children, the rest of the children must be engaged in reading and writing practice without the support of the teacher. In fact, that reality might actually be best, especially for children with strong entering profiles. So our concept of instructional diet applies not only to what is taught but how, in terms of both time and groupings.

A similar design was used to investigate the relationship between instruction and achievement in third grade. Connor, Morrison, and Petrella (2004) explored the extent to which explicit/implicit instruction, teacher-managed/child-managed, word-level/higher-order, and time were associated with achievement in comprehension. They observed instruction for 108 children in 43 classrooms in fall, winter, and spring. They found that third graders who began the year with average or below-average reading comprehension made more growth in classrooms where teachers provided more time in teacher-managed, explicit comprehension instruction (such as discussion, reading comprehension strategy instruction, instruction on conventions of text, group writing, and vocabulary instruction) and less time in child-managed explicit instruction (such as completing an individual reading comprehension activity or a group writing activity). For students who began third grade with strong comprehension scores, stronger growth came with more time in child-managed comprehension activities, including peer activities.

These two studies highlight the fact that providing children what they need maximizes their growth; one-size-fits-all instruction simply will not be as effective as differentiated instruction. We urge teachers, then, to accept the fact that the children in their classrooms are at different places along the road leading to full and meaningful literacy. Knowing where they are and where they need to go and also knowing some strategies for getting them there on time is the real heart of a differentiated instructional plan.

DIFFERENTIATION AND DEVELOPMENT

That plan is a tall order for any teacher. The design of differentiated instruction demands a high level of understanding of reading development and thoughtful attention to data. We think that the model provided recently by the RAND Reading Study Group (2002) to define comprehension is a useful one; we have reprinted it in Figure 1.4. Reading comprehension, the goal of all reading instruction, is a cognitive act of extraction and construction of meaning, an act that is influenced by characteristics of the reader, the text, and the activity or goal, each of which is influenced by multiple sociocultural contexts. You can access the full report of the study group electronically (*www.rand.org/publications/MR/MR1465/*).

During the period of reading acquisition, however, it is difficult to use such a holistic model to design instruction. Rather, researchers and teachers must break down reading comprehension and consider isolated areas for assessment and instruction. Recently, our attention has been on these areas: phonemic awareness, phonics, fluency, vocabulary, and comprehension. In this book, we consider in-

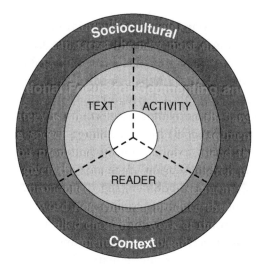

FIGURE 1.4. Heuristic for defining reading. From RAND Reading Study Group (2002). Copyright 2002 by RAND Corporation. Reprinted by permission.

structional, developmental, and assessment issues in each of these areas separately, but our goal is to equip students to integrate learning across these areas to aid in the construction of meaning. Our goal is to provide all children the means to really experience reading in school in the ways that the RAND study group has conceptualized it; our strategy for reaching that goal, however, is to take assessment data and developmental conceptions into account in deciding what part of the literacy diet to target during needs-based instructional time.

A DIFFERENTIATED DIFFERENTIATION PLAN

Even with high-quality whole-class instruction, some children will not make adequate progress. Screening and progress monitoring assessments help teachers identify those children, and thoughtful classroom instructional schedules allow for small groups of children to have additional instruction during the literacy block. The materials that follow present instructional strategies teachers can use to address the needs of these children. The instructional strategies we have chosen are based on research studies showing that their use accelerated children's literacy development. We present these strategies in five sections: phonemic awareness, phonics, fluency, vocabulary, and comprehension. Teachers may need to use strategies from more than one section to meet the needs of a group of children. For example, one group of kindergarteners may need to work on phonemic awareness and phonics. A group of first or second graders may need to work on phonics and fluency.

A group of third graders may need to work on fluency and comprehension. Crafting a flexible and responsive differentiation plan will require that teachers understand the structure of their core scope and sequence of instruction; that they use and understand continuous assessments of student progress; that, based on these data, they choose to implement specific differentiation strategies, alone or in combination; and that they select content from their core to preteach or reteach.

Sequence of instruction is key to instructional design for needs-based instruction. Oudeans (2003) recently conceptualized choices that are important to consider when combining two instructional goals (e.g., phonemic awareness and phonics; phonics and fluency; fluency and comprehension; vocabulary and comprehension). The two goals may be successive. That is, students need to master a series of lessons in one area and then they can move to the next area. The activities may be parallel. Students may be able to master both goals independently at the same time, splitting attention in half during the needs-based session. They may also be integrated, with two sets of goals driving design of the sessions, and conscious integration of the goals also apparent. We think that the last, integration, is probably the most effective and also the most difficult for teachers to realize. A truly integrated instructional plan will use time and strategies in specific domains to meet big-picture comprehension goals; that road will demand work across the grade levels to teach decoding skills, build fluency, build and activate prior knowledge, teach vocabulary words, motivate students, and engage them in personal response.

Teachers must find ways to make their instructional plans both effective and manageable. We hope that the differentiation strategies presented here advance both goals. Here are the steps that we recommend to choose and use these differentiation strategies. We are accustomed to working with teams of teachers who are reflecting together on instructional quality and making curriculum decisions. If possible, we recommend that these steps be followed in collaborative grade-level teams, with the work divided and the products and experiences shared.

Step 1: Gather Your Resources

1. Find and examine the scope and sequence of instruction in your core and supplementary materials for developing phonics skills, recognition of high-frequency words, oral vocabulary, and comprehension strategies.
2. Locate and organize any informal achievement or placement tests that are associated with your materials, looking specifically for assessments that provide evidence that children are mastering the skills and strategies targeted in the curriculum.
3. Locate and organize any informal assessments provided in texts in the school's library of professional books.

Step 2: Consider Your Children's Needs

1. Review the most recent screening data and determine whether additional informal data are needed.
2. Make instructional groups based on the data.
3. Choose two areas to target for each group (e.g., phonemic awareness and phonics, phonics and fluency, fluency and comprehension, comprehension and vocabulary).
4. Choose differentiation strategies in those areas.
5. Gather or make materials for 3 weeks of needs-based instruction.

Step 3: Try It Out!

1. Pilot your plan for 3 weeks.
2. Gather with colleagues to share, evaluate, and fine-tune differentiation plans, considering the changing needs of children and teachers.

In the chapters that follow, we will guide you through this process. We begin with assessment so that you can launch your differentiation plan with a sound assessment blueprint. Then we work through each of the areas in the literacy diet in turn. In each chapter, we provide some important background knowledge for teachers and then highlight several different strategies for differentiating in that area. Finally, we provide snapshots of differentiation in action in different classrooms in kindergarten through third grade.

CHAPTER 2

Using Assessment
to Differentiate Instruction

In Chapter 1, we put our differentiation cards on the table. The focus of this book is very specific—planning and implementing instruction for flexible small groups of students in targeted tasks with assistance from a teacher. We also challenged teachers to consider that these groups are temporary, both in terms of their membership and in terms of their focus. Since reading is a developmental process, and since we expect children's knowledge, skills, and strategies to change as a result of differentiated instruction, students will outgrow both the group itself and the focus of the instruction. Without assessment, differentiating instruction would not be possible. There are four important questions that we can answer only on the basis of information gathered through assessments:

1. Which students need additional instruction in a given area?
2. What are their specific instructional needs in this area?
3. How much progress are we making in addressing these needs?
4. How effective is the additional instruction across students?

Surprisingly, the answers to these questions do not depend on sophisticated commercial tests requiring extensive expertise to administer and interpret. Informal assessments can work just as well, so long as they are valid and reliable. That is, the measures we use must assess the curriculum we are trying to teach, and they must yield consistent results on which we can safely depend while planning instruction.

FOUR TYPES OF ASSESSMENTS

To answer the four questions above, we need four kinds of assessments. These will enable us to screen students for general deficiencies, to diagnose their specific needs, to monitor our progress in addressing these needs, and to judge the outcome of our intervention efforts for a number of students. Some assessments can be used for more than one of these purposes, while others are not so versatile. Let's take a closer look at each of the four types. Figure 2.1 provides an overview of these types of assessments and also some common tasks for each. It is our goal here to provide a conceptual model for assessment rather than to recommend specific ones. For a deeper discussion of particular assessments (including many that are available easily and cheaply) see McKenna and Stahl (2003).

Screening Measures

In order to identify children in need of intervention in an area, we rely on a screening measure. Such an instrument tells us whether a significant problem may exist in the area. Some screening measures have benchmarks to help us make this determination. We can compare a child's performance against the benchmark established for a particular grade level and time of year. For less formal screening measures, we may use "generic" benchmarks. These may derive from research studies or state standards. For example, the Georgia second-grade fluency standard states that children must be able to read aloud second-grade text at 90 words correct per minute. This is quite consistent with the benchmark established by Hasbrouck and Tindal (2006) for children at the 50th percentile rank in spring of second grade. Such benchmarks are useful indicators of achievement and enable teachers to judge how far below the expected level a child is performing. The crucial question—one requiring insightful judgment—is how far behind a child must be before differentiated instruction is warranted.

One widely used set of screening assessments, the Dynamic Indicators of Basic Early Literacy Skills (DIBELS), can serve as an illustration. If you would like to know more about DIBELS, see descriptions available at the DIBELS website (*dibels.uoregon.edu/*). In the case of DIBELS subtests, some interpretations are made for us; the data are reported in three categories (benchmark, strategic, or intensive). Children with scores in the benchmark range in an area are accomplishing adequate achievement. Children with scores in the strategic range will likely need differentiated instruction to reach benchmarks. Children with scores in the intensive range need differentiated instruction and also may need additional even more intensive instruction.

Another widely used set of screening assessments are the Phonological Awareness Literacy Screenings (PALS PreK, PALS K, and PALS 1–3). These comprehen-

Assessment type	Characteristics	Common formats
Screening	Quickly determines whether a deficit exists Provides little information about specific instructional needs within an area	Usually based on fairly advanced skill Examples: • In phonological awareness, the ability to segment a spoken word into phonemes • In phonics, the ability to pronounce nonsense words • In fluency, the ability to read aloud grade-level text at preset words correct per minute • In vocabulary, the ability to match a spoken word with a visual representation • In comprehension, the ability to read grade-level text and answer questions at more than one level
Diagnostic	Subdivides a broad area into specific skills and competencies Results directly inform instruction by identifying skills on which to focus Generally longer than screening tests *Note.* Diagnostic tests of fluency, vocabulary, and comprehension are problematic.	Could involve a complete inventory of skills, from basic to advanced Examples: • A phonics inventory might begin by having child provide sounds represented by consonant letters, then proceed to pronouncing short-vowel words, etc. • A phonological awareness inventory might begin by asking the child to tell which of three words does not rhyme with the other two, then proceed to more sophisticated tasks, such as saying a word segmented by the examiner or segmenting a word pronounced by the examiner
Progress monitoring	Quick periodic measure to determine response to treatment Often alternate form of screening test	Same form as screening tests
Outcome	Provide index of growth across many students Generally group administered Could be norm- or criterion-referenced Of little use in day-to-day instructional planning	Formats generally must be adapted for silent responses Examples: • Multiple-choice vocabulary and comprehension items Screening measures are often used as outcome measures for phonological awareness, phonics, and fluency because silent response formats are problematic

FIGURE 2.1. Characteristics and formats of the four types of assessments.

sive screening assessments are also scored with benchmarks to identify students for whom more instruction (and sometimes more diagnostic information) will be needed. For more information on these measures, see the PALS website (*pals.virginia.edu/*). In other cases (when the tests themselves do not provide benchmark or risk scores) we must rely on professional judgments to make such recommendations.

Our experience has been that the need for differentiated instruction is usually clear. Available assessments are not perfect, however, and children may be erroneously classified. There are two potential screening errors, based on the particular assessment we use or our skill at interpreting it. Sometimes a false positive will occur. In this case, we incorrectly decide that a student needs support in a given area. In the case of a false negative, on the other hand, we decide that a student has no need of extra support and instruction even though such a need exists. False positives are rare and are generally discovered quickly because students perform very well once the instruction begins. False negatives lead to delays in identifying children in need and are consequently more serious. Gaining experience in giving and interpreting screening measures is therefore important.

It is now common for screening measures to accompany a commercial core reading program. Such measures are very useful because they provide evidence of the potential match or mismatch of skills that children have and the skills assumed by the designers of the program. Teachers who do not use a comprehensive screening system should investigate whether their core offers screening tests. If so, they should become familiar with how to use them.

Diagnostic Measures

After a child has been identified for differentiated instruction through screening, further assessment is required. Generally, the screening test does not provide results that are detailed enough to actually help us plan instruction; it simply alerts the teacher to be concerned. To plan instruction, a diagnostic measure must be given. Such a measure breaks down a general area like phonics or phonemic awareness into specific skills and strategies. A child's inability to perform well in one or more of these specific areas tells us that additional, focused instruction is needed.

Diagnostic tests, despite a traditional mystique, are not necessarily hard to administer. Many are informal in nature and are relatively quick to give and score. For example, if we identify a general need for additional phonics instruction through screening, we can administer a phonics skill inventory that will quickly reveal specific deficits. Many such instruments are available and many are in the public domain. A good source of copyable diagnostic instruments in all of the major dimensions of reading is McKenna and Stahl (2003).

Progress Monitoring Measures

Once differentiated instruction begins, teachers must periodically check to see whether their efforts are paying off. Imagine a dentist who identifies a cavity, x-rays it to diagnose its exact size and shape, and then begins drilling without ever stopping to inspect the results. As absurd as this example may sound, something very similar can easily happen if we get into the habit of teaching without monitoring. The danger is that once we have identified a specific need, we may overteach to correct it. This may happen because we have access to ample materials, because we feel we must carry a particular series of lessons to a logical end, or simply because we enjoy teaching a particular skill or strategy. Progress monitoring tests can avert this problem. More importantly, they can alert us to instances where there is little or no response to the intervention so that we can adjust our approach before more time is wasted. For such tests to work properly, they must be given on a regular basis.

There is little research to help us recommend the proper frequency with which to administer progress monitoring assessments. Formal progress monitoring systems may make it possible to monitor progress on a weekly basis, but teachers can also use assessments that may accompany core materials. Conceptually, progress monitoring must be part of every differentiated lesson in that we want teachers to attend to the degree to which students are succeeding during the lesson. It is important to check whether additional progress monitoring assessments are available. If not, teachers can inspect performance on tasks a student attempts during differentiated instruction. This is called curriculum-based assessment. It might entail scores on phonics exercises, a sight word inventory, or words correct per minute occasionally computed by a teacher during oral reading.

Periodic progress monitoring tells us two things: whether the child is progressing as expected and when the diagnosed need has been addressed. Toward these ends, it is important to keep track of student performance over time. We can do so by charting progress for each of the students receiving the differentiated instruction so that a trajectory for each child can be analyzed. Figure 2.2 shows how student progress in a third-grade fluency group can be easily recorded in the form of a

Child	Words correct per minute at end of each week							
	1	2	3	4	5	6	7	8
Ken	26	31	33	40	43	51	59	60
Nora	42	40	38	43	40	44	40	39
Stephanie	31	34	34	37	36	40	41	45

FIGURE 2.2. Sample fluency chart used to monitor the progress of intervention students.

simple chart. By casual inspection, we can see that Ken has made considerable progress, that Stephanie's improvement has been more modest, and that Nora seems to have plateaued. For Nora, the fluency group has not worked. For several weeks, the need to try a different approach has been apparent, if only the teacher had studied the results of progress monitoring. Conclusions like these do not require statistical analysis. All that is needed is common sense and systematic record keeping.

Outcome Measures

Let's revisit the case of our hypothetical fluency intervention. What if nearly all of the students had trajectories like Nora's? We would be forced to conclude that our differentiated instruction is not effective *in general* and that we must try a different approach. Too often, our concern for individual students prevents us from seeing the bigger picture. This picture can only be viewed if we look *across* students.

We can do so in several ways. One is to administer a test designed to measure growth in a broad area. A year-end achievement test might be used for this purpose, but only if it is well aligned with what was taught. Another approach is to readminister the screening measure, this time as an outcome assessment. Doing so makes pre/post comparisons possible for children receiving the instruction. A third method is to use progress monitoring records to consider collectively the paths of individual children. Using this approach, we might conclude that our fluency intervention has produced positive results for two out of three children. (There are too few children in our example to employ this method fairly, of course.)

Each of these approaches has merit. Too frequently, however, no attempt whatever is made to gauge the extent to which an intervention is working. Like our hapless dentist, we may drill merrily away with no notion of whether our efforts are actually benefiting the patients. This is why the big picture matters. Inspecting the data we have from time to time in order to judge the success of instruction is an important part of reflective teaching.

PUTTING THE ASSESSMENTS TOGETHER

For an intervention to work, we must have a coherent assessment system, one that employs the various types of assessments in concert. Using the results to inform our planning is called assessment-driven instruction. We have described a decision-making model for achieving this goal (McKenna & Walpole, 2005), a model depicted as a flowchart in Figure 2.3. The coordinated use of screening, diagnostic, and progress monitoring assessments is plain to see. If a screening assessment does not reveal a problem, core instruction continues. If, however, the child is judged to be at risk in the area screened, then assessments associated with differentiated in-

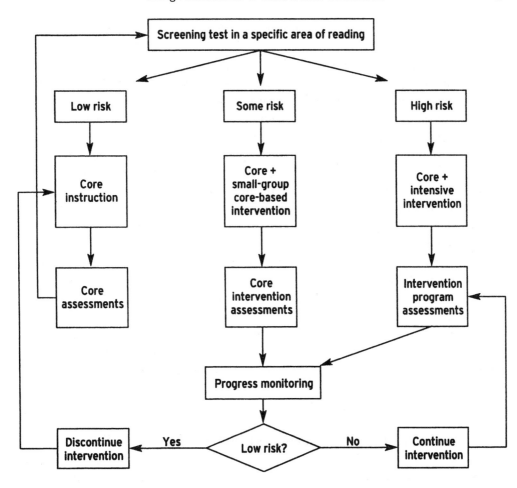

FIGURE 2.3. A model of assessment-driven instruction. From McKenna and Walpole (2005). Copyright 2005 by the International Reading Association. Reprinted by permission.

struction are administered. These are diagnostic tests, given to identify specific needs. Once the differentiated instruction is under way, progress monitoring assessments are given, and a decision is periodically made as to whether the additional instruction should continue. (As the figure indicates, the same logic applies regardless of whether the risk is determined to be moderate or great, though the intensity of the instruction will differ.)

Now let's apply this model to our fluency example. We assume that Ken has been given a screening test in oral reading fluency and that he scored well below the benchmark. Since he is a third grader, this benchmark might be 71 words correct per minute at the beginning of the year for the average student (Hasbrouck & Tindal, 2006). Ken is substantially below this level and is a clear candidate for intervention. However, that intervention might not necessarily be a fluency intervention. Diagnosing and addressing a fluency problem is a matter of investigating its component skills.

For purposes of our illustration, let's assume that Ken's phonics skills and sight word knowledge are relatively strong. This means that his principal difficulty lies in consolidating his knowledge while reading. He needs practice in applying his word recognition skills in actual reading of slightly challenging materials with teacher support. This approach constitutes the focus of differentiated instruction for him. Progress monitoring subsequently reveals steady progress, but after eight weeks he is still not reading at the beginning-of-year benchmark. Following the model, our teacher decides to continue the intervention. This same decision would be made each time the progress monitoring assessment is given as long as Ken performs well below the benchmark. When he eventually reaches it, this specific cycle of differentiated instruction will be discontinued; he may be ready to use his differentiated instruction time for working on comprehension strategies or for developing vocabulary knowledge.

You may have noted that we have made no mention of outcome measures. That is because outcome measures are not a part of the decision-making process outlined in Figure 2.2. The model pertains to an individual child. Decisions we may reach about the effectiveness of the intervention overall require information about many children and overall patterns in their response to the instruction we are providing.

DRAWING CONCLUSIONS ABOUT A CHILD'S NEEDS

In Ken's case, we had information about much more than fluency. We also knew that he was proficient in phonics and possessed good sight word knowledge. But let's change the scenario and assume that Ken was weak in phonics. In this case, our fluency screen would still indicate a problem in the area of fluency. However, an intervention based on teacher-supported oral reading practice in challenging texts could not be expected to have much effect. This is because an underlying cause of his dysfluency is not being addressed—namely, his lack of decoding skills.

In general, then, our model indicates that even if we screen in a particular area and identify a weakness, instruction in that area may not be called for. This reasoning may seem illogical. Nothing of the kind. Some reading proficiencies, such as fluency and comprehension, are actually complex clusters of skills and strategies. Poor performance on a screening test in fluency or comprehension cannot tell us which of the underlying skill sets are weak. We must systematically assess until the true picture of a child's reading becomes clear.

This systematic assessment involves a logical process guided by key questions. It is not difficult. Moreover, the questions can be addressed by data that are easily obtainable by a classroom teacher. McKenna and Stahl (2003) refer to this process as the cognitive model of reading assessment, merely because it is governed by logical reasoning based on available evidence.

There are two ways to think about the cognitive model. One is to use the flowchart depicted in Figure 2.4. This figure graphically portrays the domino-like chains of factors that result in the ability of a child to comprehend grade-level materials. Once we have evidence that a child cannot comprehend such materials, the chart requires us to track leftward along the three strands of factors until we have examined all of the possible factors contributing to the child's lack of success. The other way to think about the cognitive model is to use guiding questions associated with each box in the figure. We find that many teachers are more comfortable with this approach, perhaps because the chart has a forbidding look, but the reasoning is exactly the same.

We will now use the guiding questions to work our way through the model. Remember that our reasoning has begun with a central question—whether the child can comprehend grade-level materials—and we have answered this question negatively. We might have used a formal instrument to answer it, or an informal measure such as responding to one or more passages written at or near grade level, or repeated observations of classroom performance. Whatever the data source, we suspect that the child lags behind expectations, and the more reliable our measures, the stronger our suspicion.

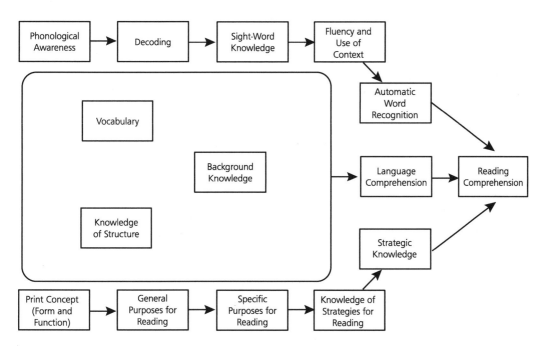

FIGURE 2.4. The cognitive model of reading assessment. From McKenna and Stahl (2003). Copyright 2003 by The Guilford Press. Reprinted by permission.

Because so many factors affect reading comprehension, we must cast a wide net if we expect to catch all of the ones that are causing a particular child's reading difficulties. We do this so that we can target our time and attention during differentiated instruction. The cognitive model requires us to pursue three separate lines of inquiry: word recognition, oral language comprehension, and strategy use. We pursue each line until the answer to the guiding question is yes—again, a somewhat counterintuitive plan.

Guiding Questions about Word Recognition

The link between word recognition and reading comprehension is the first possibility we explore. We begin with two related questions, the answers to which will tell us whether we must go further down this path.

1. *Does the child make use of context to monitor his or her reading?* Proficient readers use context as they read, but they use it differently than poor readers. Consider the following sentence:

> She signed a legal contract.

When you got to the last word, you knew the first syllable was accented because in this context *contract* must be a noun. Now try this sentence:

> As they cool, metal objects contract.

This time context helps you quickly discern that *contract* is a verb and that the second syllable must be accented. A poor reader may not use context in this way and may mispronounce the word. More importantly, the struggling reader will often attempt to use context to figure out what the word is in the first place because of poor decoding skills. Consider a beginning reader faced with this sentence:

> The cowboy rode a brown horse.

The child who substitutes *pony* for *horse* is revealing an overreliance on context. Although once thought to be evidence of mature reading, these substitutions are now recognized as attempts to compensate for decoding deficiencies.

To answer the guiding question, look to the pronunciation of multiple-meaning words, especially in cases where the more frequent pronunciation is not indicated. Also, look at the nature of words substituted during oral reading. If a child is using context to supplement weak decoding skills, other guiding questions about decoding should be addressed.

2. *Is the child fluent?* Oral reading fluency is central to comprehension because it means the child is free to train attention on understanding. Dysfluent reading indicates that the child's conscious mental resources are split between word recognition and comprehension.

To answer this guiding question, measure the number of words correct in a minute's time as a child reads an unfamiliar sample of grade-level material. Then compare this number with the normal expectation for grade and time of year. (Instructions for doing so appear in Chapter 5.) If the child's words correct per minute are substantially below the expectation, you must proceed to the following questions to determine why so that you can provide targeted instruction. On the other hand, if fluency development is a strength, you should go no further in this set of questions; instead, next consider the guiding questions concerning oral language comprehension.

3. *Does the child have adequate sight word knowledge?* A prerequisite to oral reading fluency is sight word knowledge. A child's sight vocabulary—those words that can be pronounced immediately, without conscious analysis—will limit fluency if it is not sufficiently extensive. This is because if a word is not in a child's sight vocabulary it will require conscious attention during reading—attention that might otherwise be devoted to comprehension. It is useful to consider whether the child has adequate knowledge of the words most frequently encountered in text— high-frequency words.

To answer this guiding question, use a high-frequency word inventory. Any list of high-frequency words can be administered as an inventory by asking a child to pronounce each word in isolation. Words that cannot be pronounced quickly (typically, within 1 second) are not sight words. There are no research-based norms for evaluating sight word knowledge, but common sense will enable you to classify a child as weak or strong in this area.

4. *Does the child have adequate knowledge of decoding strategies?* Even for the child with a weak sight word vocabulary, you must address this question. Remember that you have already determined that the child is not adequately fluent, and there may be two factors underlying the problem: automaticity, especially with high-frequency words, and phonics knowledge.

To answer this guiding question, look first to informal assessments provided with your core reading materials. A phonics inventory may be available to help you determine whether phonics development is behind the skill sequence to which the child has been exposed. You can also use an established informal phonics inventory (e.g., McKenna & Stahl, 2003) or make your own, perhaps using Figure 4.2 as a guide. Phonics inventories generally begin by presenting children with letters and letter combinations and ask the child to give the sounds they represent. For instance, consonant sounds might be evaluated by presenting a random array of letters like *b*, *z*, *m*, and so forth, and asking not for the letter names but for the phonemes they typically represent. ("What sound does this letter make?") The same approach can be used to identify gaps in more sophisticated phonics knowledge, such as the relationship between letters and sounds in digraphs and blends. Asking a child to pronounce real and/or nonsense words can be used to assess knowledge of vowel sounds and orthographic patterns. Keep in mind that deficiencies in these areas do not automatically indicate an instructional emphasis. First, you must address the last of the word recognition questions.

5. *Does the child have adequate phonological awareness?* Unless the child is aware of the component sounds in spoken words, learning to associate letters with those sounds will be a difficult task. In other words, phonological awareness provides a bootstrap to aid in the learning of phonics concepts. This means that it is not enough to identify a deficit in phonics. You must also determine whether the deficit is exacerbated by poor phonological awareness. If not, phonics instruction is called for. If so, teaching phonological awareness, perhaps in conjunction with phonics, must be the first order of business. The age and receptiveness of the student must also be considered in determining whether to attempt phonological awareness instruction with older students.

To answer this guiding question, look again to the availability of core assessments. These will take the child through a sequence of experiences, from basic to sophisticated. Chapter 3 outlines this sequence as a progression from the ability to tell whether two spoken words are the same or different (*cat ≠ pat*) to the ability to segment a spoken word into phonemes (*cat* = /k/ /a/ /t/). Figure 3.1 provides the full progression of tasks. These tasks can be easily posed so that you can quickly get a good idea of a struggling child's phonological awareness.

Guiding Questions about Oral Language Comprehension

Regardless of how the word recognition questions are answered, you must address the issue of language comprehension. This is because problems may exist in both areas. Identifying a decoding problem, for example, is not the end of the assessment process, for even though addressing that problem will clearly help, it may be necessary to provide needs-based instruction on a wider front.

1. *Does the child have adequate vocabulary for age and grade?* We are referring to listening vocabulary, a concept that does not depend on the child's ability to recognize printed words. Unless word meanings are accessible as the child reads, decoding is meaningless and comprehension will be constrained or even prevented altogether.

To answer this guiding question, good observational skills are imperative. The National Reading Panel (National Institute of Child Health and Human Development, 2000) observed that assessing vocabulary knowledge is a haunting limitation in our ability to determine the instructional needs of children. Formal vocabulary testing can be informative but also prohibitively long. Our experience is that informal, curriculum-based assessments can be useful in identifying children whose limited listening vocabularies pose a threat to their comprehension development. By curriculum based, we mean being in tune during instruction to possible problems a child may experience owing to limited vocabulary knowledge. For example, a read-aloud might provide a context for a teacher to ask questions about specific words, especially words likely to be known to students at a particular grade level. Because the teacher has read the selection aloud, weak decoding cannot be blamed for lack of word knowledge. It is also important to *listen* as children speak, judging over time the extent of word knowledge they bring with them to class. While assessment of vocabulary is problematic in a formal sense, it is fairly easy to determine whether it represents a substantial deficit.

2. *Does the child have background knowledge necessary to comprehend a particular passage?* Experiences and general funds of knowledge are not quite the same as vocabulary. Limited prior knowledge, whether or not we express it as word knowledge, invariably influences comprehension. For a specific selection, ignorance of factual information that the author *assumes* the reader knows will pose a significant pitfall for any reader. Consider this passage:

> It was the day of the big party. Mary wondered if Johnny would like a kite. She ran to her bedroom, picked up her piggy bank, and shook it. There was no sound. (Eskey, 2002)

The author assumes that the reader brings certain background knowledge to the reading situation and that it is therefore not necessary to explain that a *birthday* party is referred to, that it is Johnny's birthday, that guests are expected to bring presents, that a kite might make a good present in this case, or that a piggy bank is used by a child to store money. While Eskey offered the example to illustrate the particular problems faced by English language learners who encounter culturally unfamiliar content, similar difficulties could confront any reader.

To answer the guiding question, you must determine whether limited background knowledge is likely to pose a problem. One way of doing so is to ask postreading questions that target assumptions made by an author about what the reader can be expected to know ("What kind of party was this?"). Another approach is to anticipate prior knowledge deficits conservatively and then build background extensively prior to reading a passage aloud. Alternating your approach—that is, heavy background building on one occasion, little on the next—can reveal a deficit if comprehension is improved by heavy attention to background.

3. *Is the child able to use text structures to aid comprehension?* Proficient readers know that not all selections are structured in the same way. Genres differ in the way they are typically organized. A biography is built differently from a

piece of realistic fiction or an explanation, and knowing how each is structured can aid comprehension. This is why systematically exposing children to a variety of genres is important to their becoming proficient comprehenders.

To answer this guiding question, ask questions that reveal structural knowledge. For example, write all but the last word of a limerick on the board and ask what that word might be. Or pause at a predictable point in a read-aloud and ask what might happen next, or how the child might continue the story. An alternative is to examine written work for structural components. Remember, of course, that children cannot be expected to anticipate structures to which they have not been exposed. What we are suggesting again is the use of informal, curriculum-based assessments.

Guiding Questions about Strategic Knowledge

Proficient readers do not apply the same strategies to all reading tasks. Instead, they have a sense of purpose that permits them to decide on the most appropriate way to proceed. At an absurdly obvious level, they do not read the classified ads in the same way that they read a novel. A more subtle distinction is between reading fiction and nonfiction. It is important for teachers to determine whether a child has a differentiated sense of purpose.

1. *Does the child have a set of strategies to achieve different purposes?* It takes much time and numerous, varied experiences to develop a repertoire of strategies. Struggling readers (those who have difficulty comprehending grade-level text) may have few strategies at their command. In fact, they may have only one (e.g., read and underline difficult words), to which they resort no matter what the reading selection may require. Since strategy know-how develops gradually, it is important to judge a particular child in terms of age-appropriate expectations.

To answer this guiding question, talk to the child about reading. You can use structured interviews (e.g., McKenna & Stahl, 2003), or you can speak less formally, perhaps showing the child some selections and asking how he or she might proceed. You might also ask postreading questions that are likely to reveal limited strategy use.

2. *What does the child view as the goal of reading in general?* A child who applies a limited number of strategies to all reading situations may have a skewed notion of the nature of reading and its general purpose. Too often, we find that the general purpose of reading in the mind of the struggling student is to get to the last word. It is little wonder that meaningful engagement with the content of a selection may be minimal.

To answer this guiding question, informal interviews can again be used. Questions like the following can go far toward telling you if the child possesses a good notion of the general purpose of reading:

What makes someone a good reader?
What do you do if you don't understand something?
What makes something hard to read?

3. *What concepts of print does the child have?* At the most basic level, a child, especially a very young child, may lack an adequate notion of how print works. A child with little idea of the purpose of reading may also have limited conceptualization of printed language. We find that this is rarely the case after the first grade, but it is a possibility that should not be ignored.

To answer this guiding question, structured observation is helpful. With an open book between you and the child, ask where the words are and where you would start reading. Have the child trace a finger along the first line and then move it to the beginning of the next line. Place two note cards on the page and demonstrate how they can be pushed together to reveal less print or spread apart to show more. Ask the child to slide the cards together until one word is visible. Then one letter. These tasks can quickly reveal whether print concepts are firm. In sum, the following concepts are crucial to understanding how English print functions. Each can be readily assessed informally:

- Letter boundaries
- Word boundaries
- Left-to-right directionality
- Top-to-bottom directionality, with return sweep
- Front-to-back directionality for multiple-page texts.

We find that teachers know that print concepts are important, but they do not always use assessment data to determine whether or not to teach them during differentiated instruction. In fact, we often see teachers using valuable small-group time to teach print concepts that their students have clearly already mastered.

FORMING FLEXIBLE GROUPS BASED ON ASSESSED NEEDS

The guiding questions can help ensure that key possibilities are not overlooked and that the assessment process is systematic and efficient. Remember that we began this chapter by introducing the concepts of screening, diagnosis, and progress monitoring as essential to our differentiation plan. We encourage you to find and use screening tools that rule out the need for further investigation of the skills of your proficient readers; we do not intend for you to use all assessments for all children. If you follow the cognitive model thoroughly for your struggling readers, though, you may find that the same child would benefit from instruction in more than one group. For example, a child may have both a limited knowledge of phonics and an inadequate listening vocabulary. It is up to you to decide what groups to form, based on your classroom's overall profile of assessed needs and on your ability to schedule and manage multiple groups. In later chapters we will describe ways to plan small-group lessons so as to combine in a single lesson two needs shared by members of the same group.

We conclude this chapter with strategies for ensuring that a particular needs-based group has been formed by following the cognitive model. We will not discuss the possibility of forming multiple groups, or of combining areas to be addressed for the same group. To complement our discussion, we offer a quick-reference chart for later use (see Figure 2.5). This chart captures the key ideas in checklist form. Keep in mind that in using the chart you may be referred from one portion of it to another. As you work through the rest of the chapters in this book, we hope you might return to this one to deepen your understanding of the need for a sound and efficient assessment blueprint.

Forming Word Recognition Groups

When There Is a Problem with Fluency

When screening reveals a deficit in oral reading fluency (e.g., by applying the criteria presented in Figure 5.2), screening in sight vocabulary and phonics is necessary before establishing a needs-based group in fluency. If sight vocabulary and phonics are adequate, then the child's apparent problem lies in integrating word recognition skills at an automatic level, and the instructional strategies described in Chapter 5 are likely to bear fruit.

When There Is a Problem with Sight Vocabulary

When a sight word inventory has revealed that the child cannot recognize many high-frequency words (e.g., an inventory based on the words in Figure 4.3), a needs-based group can be formed and instruction can be planned to teach the specific words that children do not know. Because a limited sight vocabulary does not imply adequate phonics knowledge, however, screening in the area of phonics is also indicated; teachers might find that they can form groups for students who need instruction in both areas.

When There Is a Problem with Phonics

When screening reveals a deficit in the acquisition of decoding skills, your first impulse may be to provide small-group instruction in this area, following diagnostic assessment of the specific skills needed. However, you should first be sure that an underlying problem in phonological awareness can be ruled out. If it can, then an

Word recognition		
Deficit revealed by screening	*Next steps . . .*	
Oral reading fluency	• Screen in phonics. • If there is a problem in phonics, do not group for fluency. • Screen for sight vocabulary (see Figure 4.3). • If there is a problem in sight vocabulary, do not group for fluency. • If phonics and sight vocabulary are adequate, provide fluency instruction. • See Chapter 5 for suggested instructional strategies.	
Sight vocabulary	• Screen in phonics. • Plan needs-based sight word instruction based on words inventoried. • See Chapter 4 for suggested instructional strategies.	
Phonics	• Screen in phonological awareness. • If there is a problem in phonological awareness, do not group for phonics. • Give a phonics inventory to determine specific deficits (see Figure 4.2). • Provide targeted phonics instruction. • See Chapter 4 for suggested instructional strategies.	
Phonological awareness	• Give a phonological awareness inventory. • Use the inventory to determine the level of awareness (see Figure 3.1). • Provide instruction designed to bring the child to the next level. • See Chapter 3 for suggested instructional strategies.	
Language comprehension		
Deficit revealed by screening	*Next steps . . .*	
Vocabulary	• Identify useful, unfamiliar words in a read-aloud or core selection. • Provide instruction in these words, using the selection for context. • See Chapter 6 for suggested instructional strategies. • Consider serving vocabulary and knowledge problems in the same group.	
Background knowledge	• Conduct prereading questioning to determine gaps in prior knowledge. • Provide prereading instruction as needed to fill such gaps. • Consider serving vocabulary and knowledge problems in the same group.	
Text structures	• Conduct prereading discussion to determine knowledge of a selection's structure. • Provide instruction in the organizational pattern if needed.	
Strategy use		
Deficit revealed by screening	*Next steps . . .*	
Comprehension strategies	• Screen in the goal of reading. • If there is a problem realizing this goal, begin by addressing that problem. • If child realizes the goal of reading, assess strategies diagnostically, using the list appearing in Figure 7.2. • Provide instruction in strategies where proficiency is limited. • See Chapter 7 for suggested instructional strategies.	
Goal of reading	• Screen for concepts of print. • If there is a problem with concepts of print, begin by addressing it. • If concepts of print are firm, provide instruction in the goal of reading.	
Concepts of print	• Conduct diagnostic assessment using list of concepts on page 25. • Provide instruction in how print functions.	

FIGURE 2.5. Checklist for Forming Needs-Based Groups.

inventory of phonics skills, perhaps based on the listing in Figure 4.2, can inform your instructional planning.

When There Is a Problem with Phonological Awareness

Once you have determined through screening that a problem exists, identify the level of awareness that the child has attained. Figure 3.1 can help you pinpoint this level. You should begin instruction at the *next* level with the goal of helping the child reach it. Because phonological awareness is the bedrock skill of word recognition, it is not necessary to conduct further screening in other areas of word recognition.

Forming Language Comprehension Groups

When There Is a Problem with Vocabulary

When screening (either observational or formal) has revealed a deficit in listening vocabulary, diagnostic testing in the conventional sense is not possible. This is because there are too many words for children to know, and specific word knowledge cannot be comprehensively assessed. However, you can easily identify unfamiliar Tier 2 words in a read-aloud or core selection and build knowledge of their meanings. Determining which words to teach serves the purpose of diagnostic assessment. If you are using a developmental vocabulary program, of course, diagnostic assessments may be available to help determine unfamiliar words.

When There Is a Problem with Background Knowledge

As in the case of vocabulary, when your observation identifies background knowledge as a factor limiting a child's comprehension, conventional diagnostic assessment is not conducted. Instead, background building prior to reading or listening is done whenever you suspect that the author assumes knowledge that the child is unlikely to possess. You may gauge such knowledge by posing prereading questions designed to determine such gaps. In a very real sense, such questions constitute diagnostic assessment. Keep in mind that because vocabulary and background knowledge are highly correlated, you may wish to combine needs-based grouping in addressing these problems. Keep in mind that they are problems addressed repeatedly, for each new selection. Indeed, limited vocabulary and background knowledge are slow to yield to instructional intervention.

When There Is a Problem with Text Structures

When your observation indicates that a child is generally unfamiliar with a variety of text structures, diagnostic assessment must focus on the structure of each new reading selection. By conducting a prereading (or prelistening) discussion, you can determine whether the selection's organizational pattern is familiar to the child. A needs-based group designed to address such a deficit may be short-lived since such patterns are usually easy to teach.

Forming Strategic Knowledge Groups

When There Is a Problem with Comprehension Strategies

When a structured interview reveals that the child has few strategies to use in comprehending text, the next step is to determine whether the child has a firm knowledge of the general goal of reading, which is to get meaning from print. If the child possesses this understanding, diagnostic strategy assessment is couched within selections to be read and within read-alouds. You can quickly determine a child's proficiency at applying specific strategies by asking questions during and after the selection. You can use the list of strategies in Figure 7.2 as a guide for asking questions and posing tasks. If you determine that a child has limited proficiency in a particular strategy, direct explanation in a small-group setting is appropriate.

When There Is a Problem Understanding the Goal of Reading

When your questioning reveals that a child does not have a clear idea of the goal of reading, you must first check to see if the child has an adequate notion of how print functions. If print concepts are strong, then small-group instruction in the proper goal of reading (comprehension!), salted with plenty of good examples, is appropriate.

When There Is a Problem with Concepts of Print

When observation indicates that a child may not fully understand how print functions, a diagnostic session is called for in which you present a series of tasks to determine where understanding is weak. A list of such tasks appears earlier in this chapter. Because concepts of print represent a bedrock proficiency that grounds more advanced strategy use, poor performance on these tasks does not require screening in any other area.

A FINAL WORD

What about your children who are achieving at or above grade level? We do not leave them out of our model, and we do not want teachers to leave them out of differentiated small-group instruction. Such students will benefit from instructional activities that challenge them to reach their potential. With the strong national focus on struggling readers, it is easy to lose sight of the needs of abler students. However, the instruction they receive is equally important, and addressing their needs is a crucial part of our efforts to differentiate instruction.

Using assessments to form needs-based groups is not an exact science and we are glad of that! We have provided guidelines for making the best use of available information about children and about how to obtain more information when it is needed to make important instructional decisions. Keep in mind, however, that assessment results are always imperfect—they merely estimate the proficiencies we wish to target. Be flexible about reacting to student performance if it seems to contradict what you thought you knew about a child. Your experiences interacting with children once a needs-based group is formed may cause you to reconsider your initial conclusions. You are, after all, the final arbiter of a child's instructional needs. Assessments should guide your judgments, not make them for you.

CHAPTER 3

Differentiating Phonemic Awareness Instruction

As children begin their formal schooling, their motivation to learn to read is high. Their parents are hopeful that they will master early literacy skills on schedule, and, in fact, their success in school depends on it. Many children will attain early literacy skills during kindergarten and first grade seemingly without effort, but others will not. One thing that those children who struggle with early literacy have in common is weak phonemic awareness. Teachers who know how to differentiate can provide instruction that goes a long way toward mediating that struggle.

Phonemic awareness, while not a perfect predictor of literacy success, appears to exert a strong influence on its early development. This is not surprising since in an alphabetic language like English, understanding how it works depends on becoming aware of the smallest sounds that make up spoken words. These building blocks of spoken words are phonemes. Phonemic awareness is the ability to hear, identify, and manipulate the individual sounds in spoken words. A kindergarten child with strong phonemic awareness can tell you that the word *pet* is composed of three phonemes: /p/ /e/ /t/. If that child also knows how to write letters, he or she can produce strong invented spellings of virtually any word, and can read many phonetically regular words by sounding and blending. A seminal study in this area traced the literacy progress of 54 children, most from low-income homes, from kindergarten through fourth grade. Those children who began first grade with weak phonemic awareness skills had a .88 probability of remaining below-grade-level readers in fourth grade (Juel, 1988). Given that resources for intervention are sparse in the upper elementary grades, the prognosis for readers who reach those grades without sufficient skills and strategies for reading to learn is not promising.

Juel's study drew attention to the importance of early success in phonemic awareness, and there is ample evidence that almost all children can attain this basic skill. The prognosis for success with developing phonemic awareness is very good for most children. In fact, many teachers have developed the assessment skills to identify children who need phonemic awareness instruction and the instructional skills to provide such instruction in differentiated small-group instruction. In this chapter, we summarize important research in this area and describe simple procedures that teachers can use to provide differentiated instruction in phonemic awareness. Our recommendations in this chapter are most appropriate for kindergarten and early first grade.

The highest-profile research review in the area of phonemic awareness was produced by the National Reading Panel (NRP). The panel was convened by Congress to summarize research in the areas of phonemic awareness, phonics and decoding, fluency, vocabulary, comprehension, and teacher education. The panel's charge was to combine the results of rigorous research studies (those studies employing a treatment and a control) to highlight findings with sufficient rigor for them to inform all classroom instruction. In 2000, the NRP released its findings and they are available in full online at no cost (*www.nationalreadingpanel.org/Publications/publications.htm*). In addition, two simpler documents, also available online at the same site, translate the findings for teachers: *Put Reading First: The Research Building Blocks for Teaching Children to Read* (Armbruster, Lehr, & Osborn, 2001) and for parents: *Put Reading First: Helping Your Child Learn to Read* (National Institute for Literacy).

The NRP report highlighted the positive long-term effects of phonemic awareness instruction. This instruction improves decoding, spelling, and comprehension. While there are many potential tasks that constitute phonemic awareness instruction, two are most powerful: blending and segmenting. That finding is intuitively sensible. Blending sounds is essential in decoding new words and segmenting sounds is essential in spelling them. Phonemic awareness interventions that include letters, and that therefore connect speech sounds with the letters representing them, are more effective than interventions that use only oral activities. The NRP also found that small-group work was more powerful than whole-group instruction and even more effective than tutoring. Phonemic awareness is the perfect place to start as we consider strategies for differentiating instruction.

RECENT RESEARCH AND REVIEWS

Not all educators embraced the findings of the NRP. In fact, this particular section of the report generated substantial negative reaction. Educators and policy makers tended to overreact to the panel's report, speculating that integrated kindergarten literacy activities would be replaced by mindless drilling of sounds. Such potential misrepresentations of the panel's findings should be resisted. However, ignoring the panel's findings is equally unwise. We know of no studies that have contradicted the basic findings reported by the NRP; phonemic awareness aids literacy development and it can be developed by teachers during regular classroom instruction.

Since the NRP report, researchers have continued to explore the developmental nature of phonemic awareness. Phonemic awareness is the most advanced stage of phonological awareness. Phonological awareness is an umbrella term that encompasses rhyme and syllable awareness, onset–rime awareness, and phoneme awareness. Anthony and Lonigan (2004) have tried to understand how these various forms of phonological awareness are related. Generally, they found that all phonological sensitivities, including larger-unit rhyme sensitivity and smaller-unit phoneme sensitivity, are related, and that various assessment measures could be used to identify children for prevention-based instruction.

The design and organization of that prevention-based instruction is important. Oudeans (2003) carefully considered instructional sequence in a kindergarten phonemic awareness program. Her treatment group included kindergarten nonreaders. The children worked in groups of three to four for 15 minutes each day over 10 weeks. For all children, half of their instruction was direct instruction in oral phoneme segmentation and blending and half included direct instruction in letter names and sounds. In one treatment, these two segments of instruction were integrated. The letters taught in the "phonics" portion of the lesson were also used in the words taught in the oral segmentation and blending section. For example, the children might blend or segment the words *man, pan, fan, can,* and *ran.* Then they would review and practice letter names and sounds for *a, m, n, p, f, c, r.* In the other treatment, the letter name–letter sound lessons and the oral segmentation and blending lessons were independent of one another. The oral segmentation and blending activities might include the words *pig, rat, lip, men,* and *sack* while the letter-sound work still included *a, m, n, p, f, c,* and *r.*

Both groups made significant progress in letter name fluency (the ability to quickly produce letter names, given a random list), phoneme segmentation fluency (the ability to quickly decompose spoken words into their constituent sounds), letter sounds (the ability to produce the most common sound associated with a letter), nonsense word fluency (the ability to decode three-phoneme nonsense words, e.g., *jat, nup*), and real word reading. Children in the integrated group had greater rates of growth in these measures and also read more real words at the end of the treatment. Thus both treatments were successful in general in building these lower-level skills, but the planned integration of phonics information and oral segmentation and blending helped the children transfer these skills to real-word reading.

Teachers may be inundated with choices of commercial materials that claim to include "everything needed" to develop phonemic awareness. We have recently read a useful study that focused attention on the characteristics of such commercial curriculum materials. Santi, Menchetti, and Edwards (2004) reviewed phonemic awareness materials looking for the following characteristics: inclusion of all materials, direction about group size, supplementary activities, direction about time for instruction, modeling, and sequencing of tasks from easier to more difficult, use of letters, focus on blending and segmenting, provision of pronunciation guides for teachers, assessment criteria to indicate mastery and pacing, specific feedback techniques, review and practice, and suggestions for adapting instruction. None of the programs they reviewed was perfect, but consideration of these dimensions appears very useful for schools reviewing new programs or improving implementation and effectiveness of existing programs.

FOUNDATIONAL TEACHER KNOWLEDGE

No program of phonemic awareness activities will be perfect for all children; teachers must make important decisions at the level of implementation. As with most aspects of beginning reading instruction, understanding and implementing effective phonemic awareness instruction demands developmental knowledge. In order to teach phonemic awareness effectively and to design instruction that differentiates for the different levels of phonological awareness that children bring to school, teachers have to have an understanding of the order in which individuals typically acquire these skills. In 1999, Simmons and Kame'enui released curriculum maps to trace instructional goals in beginning reading (*reading.uoregon.edu/appendices/maps.php*). These maps included specific accomplishments in phonemic awareness across the kindergarten and first-grade years. Figure 3.1 lists them in the order in which they are first presented in the curriculum maps. Keep in mind, however, that many of these accomplishments are achieved at about the same time by individual children and that others may take several months to actually master.

There are two practical issues in providing differentiated phonemic awareness instruction. One is the unit. Larger units are easier than smaller units. For example, work with syllables is easier than work with onset and rime, and work with onset and rime is easier than work with individual phonemes. Also, fewer units are easier than more. For instance, two phonemes (e.g., in *go* or *up*) are easier to segment or blend than three (e.g., in *pin* or *map*), and working with three units is easier than working with four (e.g., in *flat* or *spin*). The second generic issue is the actual instructional tasks. Again, some are easier than others. Tolman (2005) recently summarized basic instructional procedures for the development of phonemic awareness. She created a table (adapted below in Figure 3.2) that is organized from the simplest tasks to the most complex. Research indicates that blending and

- Tells whether words and sounds are the same or different.
- Identifies whether words rhyme.
- Claps words in sentences.
- Identifies which word in a set is different.
- Produces a word that rhymes.
- Claps syllables in words.
- Identifies which speech sound is different in a set of sounds.
- Orally blends syllables or onset–rimes.
- Segments syllables.
- Identifies first sound in words.
- Orally blends individual phonemes.
- Segments individual sounds in words.
- Identifies final sounds in words.
- Blends three to four phenomes into words.
- Segments three- to four-phoneme words.
- Identifies medial sound in one-syllable words.

FIGURE 3.1. Development of phonological awareness skills as presented in Simmons and Kame'enui's (1999) curriculum maps for kindergarten and first grade.

Phoneme awareness examples		
Phoneme isolation/identity	What is the first speech sound in these words?	*giraffe, jar, jaunt*
	What is the last speech sound in these words?	*stem, comb, autumn*
Phoneme categorization	What word does not belong here?	*ceiling, kite, sister*
Phoneme blending	Blend the following sounds to make a word.	/u/ /p/, /p/ /a/ /t/, /c/ /l/ /a/ /p/
Phoneme segmenting	What are the sounds in this word?	*no, pan, clean*
Phoneme deletion	Say ____. Say ____ without the ____.	climb—/l/ = lime, clap—/l/ = lap
Phoneme addition	What word would you have if you added ____ to ____?	/sh/ + out = shout, frog + /z/ = frogs
Phoneme substitution	Say ____. Change the ____ to ____.	fish—/f/ + /d/ = dish
Phoneme reversal	Say ____. Say the sounds backwards.	ticks—skit

FIGURE 3.2. Instructional procedures for developing phonemic awareness. Adapted from Tolman (2005). Copyright 2005 by the International Dyslexia Association. Adapted by permission of Carol Tolman.

Sample item	Confusing unit	Segmentation
black	consonant blend	/b/ /l/ /a/ /ck/
thin	consonant digraph	/ch/ /i/ /n/
bu**m**p	nasal	/b/ /u/ /m/ /p/
fi**r**st	r-controlled vowel	/f/ /ir/ /s/ /t/
sn**ow**	long vowel	/s/ /n/ /ow/
b**oy**	diphthong	/b/ /oy/

FIGURE 3.3. Phoneme counting practice.

segmenting (shaded tasks in the figure) are the most important and that the importance of tasks more difficult than those is still not entirely clear.

In order to build phonemic awareness in children, you need to be able to segment phonemes yourself. This may not be as easy as it sounds. There are a few
things about phoneme segmentation that are a bit difficult for skilled readers who
already know how to read and spell virtually all words. The key concept to know
is that while English is an alphabetic language, not all phonemes are represented
by one and only one letter. Rather, each of the 44 phonemes in English might be
represented by many different graphemes. The word *though* has many letters, but
only two phonemes—the digraph sound /th/ and the long vowel sound /o/. Figure
3.3 presents some common words to help teachers remember how to count specific phonetic elements with children; the examples consistute the units that are
sometimes confusing to both teachers and children.

Next we turn our attention to several specific research-based instructional
procedures that could easily form a foundation for differentiated phonemic awareness instruction in a kindergarten or first-grade classroom. This instruction would
only constitute 10 or 15 minutes of the literacy block and would be best delivered
to small groups, perhaps four to five children. As with all instructional tasks in
this book, we envision only some children needing this instruction at all, others
needing it for a part of the year, and a few needing more time.

INITIAL SOUND SORTING

Initial sound sorting is a simple first step toward differentiated phonemic awareness instruction. It is a simple, repetitive procedure meant to help children with
very weak phonological skills begin to develop them. It is an oral-only activity;
children work only with pictures, not printed words. It can be used effectively
from very early in kindergarten, at the same time that children are learning their
alphabet.

What Kind of Reader Will Initial Sound Sorting Help?

Initial sound sorting is the first step toward phonemic awareness. It is appropriate for kindergarten children who come to school with very weak phonological awareness. They are likely to be identified as at risk on measures of letter name fluency or on phonemic awareness screenings. Even without such assessments, it is simple to determine who needs initial sound sorting—children who cannot accomplish it independently need to work on it. Teachers can easily screen an entire class of children during the first week of kindergarten by simply engaging them in small-group initial sound sorting. Those who can do it should move on to more complex tasks; those who cannot do it can begin here. Children who need to work on initial sound sorting generally have very little knowledge of letter names or letter sounds; such instruction can easily be reinforced and combined with sorting activities.

What Is the Instructional Focus for Initial Sound Sorting?

The focus of this strategy is on phoneme isolation, identification, and categorization. Given a set of pictures of familiar objects, children are guided to pronounce full words, isolate the initial consonant sounds of those words, produce those sounds, and categorize the words by their common initial sounds by physically sorting the pictures into rows or piles of pictures with the same initial sound.

Where Does Initial Sound Sorting Come from?

Initial sound sorting is difficult to attribute to any one research team. This strategy is used in many, many emergent reading programs and in many instructional interventions. However, an especially useful text for preparing and implementing the strategy is Bear, Invernizzi, Templeton, and Johnston's (2004, 4th ed.) *Words Their Way: Word Study for Phonics, Vocabulary, and Spelling Instruction*. We like this text in particular because it includes a scope and sequence for instruction that is based on the research on children's spelling development and because it includes pictures that teachers can duplicate and use directly for the instruction. Many teachers choose to duplicate the pictures on tagboard; some choose to laminate them for additional durability.

What Materials Are Needed for Initial Sound Sorting?

Work with young learners' development of phonemic awareness is much easier to accomplish with manipulates. For this strategy to work well, you need one set of picture cards for modeling, preferably large-sized so that the children can see them easily, and identical smaller sets of cards for each child to use. A full set of picture cards, with at least six to represent each initial consonant sound, can be prepared in advance. The pictures must be familiar to the children—if they cannot name the pictures, then they cannot focus their attention on the sounds. The pictures can include items that are spelled with long vowels and short vowels, and need not be only one syllable. The only thing to avoid is initial consonant blends—the initial sound in *bag* or *book* is easier to isolate than the initial sound in *black*.

We have seen teachers use many strategies for organizing their materials. Some teachers choose to keep their pictures for each initial sound in separate plastic baggies or library pockets by initial sound. Others keep the sorts together, combining pictures for a set of three different sounds and then filing them together. We favor planful organization of instructional materials; teachers should not waste time and energy each year making new materials when they can use the same ones repeatedly.

How Do You Prepare for Initial Sound Sorting?

Gone (we hope) are the days when teachers develop alphabet knowledge in order of the alphabet, one letter at a time, one letter per week. Such a strategy is neither efficient nor prudent; children would not know all of their letters until the last nine weeks of school, and there is no mechanism for review. The same concept applies to initial sound sorting. If you gave children pictures of a can, a cat, a car, and a cookie, no sorting would be necessary—all start with the same initial sound. Rather, you teach and review the letter names and sounds in small sets, including periodic review of previous sounds. Initial sound sorting is planned comparison and contrast of sets of three sounds. For example, you might begin with a set of 18 pictures representing the initial sounds for *b*, *m*, and *s*.

The key to preparing for initial sound sorting is to decide exactly which sounds to compare and contrast. In the initial sessions, compare and contrast only two sounds so that children learn how to accomplish the instructional task. Then build to three letter sounds for the remainder of the initial consonants. A good strategy for connecting initial sound sorting to the rest of the literacy curriculum in the classroom is to simply use the scope and sequence of the letter-sound instruction to organize the initial sound sorts.

How Do You Implement Initial Sound Sorting?

As with all instruction in differentiated groups, teacher modeling and repetitive instructional procedures are important. For initial sound sorting, introduce one picture to provide a target for each day's sounds. In a b/m/r sort, those might be a bag, a mit, and a rat. Isolate the first sound in those pictures repeatedly, and have children repeat chorally. Say, "Today we are going to work with words that have different beginning sounds. Some of our words will sound like /b/ *bag*, /b/ *bag*, /b/ *bag*. Say that with me. /b/ *bag*. Others will sound like /m/ *mit*, /m/ *mit*, /m/ *mit*. Say that sound with me. /m/ *mit*. The rest of the words we will work with sound like /r/ *rat*, /r/ *rat*, /r/ *rat*. Say that one with me. /r/ *rat*." Then introduce the first additional picture for the day. Say, "Does *mop* start like *bag* or like *mit* or like *rat*?"

At first, you will want to model the entire sorting procedure, with children participating, and then to ask the children to sort their own cards. Such instruction is necessary for children who are acquiring initial phoneme segmentation skills. Through modeling you make clear for children what is to be learned and how to accomplish instructional tasks. Children then can work independently, with feedback from you, to repeat the sorting procedure with their own set of manipulatives. Remember to make clear the word that is represented by each picture. What is obviously a rat to you may be seen as a mouse by the children.

How Do You Know If Initial Sound Sorting Is Working?

You will know if this strategy is working when children can sort pictures by initial sounds quickly and independently. No real testing is necessary to determine effectiveness. Remember that we are not asking children to read or spell these words; we are simply asking them to say the word aloud, isolate the initial consonant sound, and group pictures of words that begin with like sounds. Children who are no longer benefiting from differentiated instruction in initial phoneme segmentation will be able to sort picture cards easily from any set of three initial consonants.

SEGMENTING AND BLENDING

What Kind of Reader Will Segmenting and Blending Help?

Once children have learned to segment and categorize initial sounds, they can move to more complex and comprehensive phonemic awareness tasks. Most kindergarteners will benefit initially from instruction in phoneme segmentation and blending, at least at some level. Segmentation is a more difficult task than blending, so it is useful to assess segmentation first—for children who are successful at segmentation tasks, it is safe to assume that blending is not a problem and that differentiated instruction is not needed in this area. Phoneme segmentation screening data are useful in identifying students most at risk. In such assessments, children are provided oral words or pictures and asked to say the sounds in those words. Once you determine that a student needs to work on segmenting sounds, it is useful to find out where to start. Broader phonological awareness measures will be useful in determining the language units (syllables, onset–rime, phoneme) that any one individual is able to manipulate. If you know which unit a child can manipulate, your instruction can target the next most difficult unit.

What Is the Instructional Focus for Segmenting and Blending?

The focus of this strategy is on orally manipulating the language units necessary for reading (blending speech sounds) and spelling (segmenting speech sounds). Given sounds that you pronounce orally, children blend the sounds to produce words. For example, given the sounds /p/ /i/ /g/, children produce the word *pig*. Given words that you pronounce orally, children segment the words into sounds. For example, given the word *pot*, children produce three sounds: /p/ /o/ /t/. For children who are not yet skilled enough to work at the level of the phoneme, you can focus on larger units for segmenting and blending tasks. Children can segment and blend syllables (e.g., *cow-boy*) or onsets and rimes (e.g., /m/ /an/).

Where Does Segmenting and Blending Come from?

Like initial phoneme sorting, segmenting and blending is a fairly ubiquitous strategy. We can see it used in almost all commercial phonemic awareness programs and almost all phonemic awareness interventions.

What Materials Are Needed for Segmenting and Blending?

The only real materials that you need to facilitate oral segmenting and blending activities during differentiated instruction are lists of words. We encourage you to actually make lists in advance (rather than simply trying to think of words during instruction) because such thinking wastes instructional time. In the course of an hour you can make many lists of words. At the level of the syllable, the simplest words are compounds (e.g., *cowboy, backpack, lunchbox*). The next most complex would be two-syllable words (e.g., *baby, pencil, marker*). Slightly more difficult are three-syllable words (e.g., *elephant, telephone, butterfly*). Children who can blend and segment at the level of the syllable should immediately move to the onset–rime level, where any three-phoneme words will do (e.g., *m-an, t-en, p-ig, h-ot, c-up*). Children who can segment and blend at the onset–rime level should work at the phoneme level. At the level of the phoneme, the simplest lists would consist of two-phoneme words (e.g., *so, low, be, me, we, my, hi, buy, say, day*). Note that we are counting the sounds rather than the letters—this strategy will be used orally, without reading or spelling, to develop phonemic awareness. Three-phoneme words are more difficult and could be organized in many different ways: by word families (e.g., *cat, mat, sat, rat, fat, pat, hat, bat*) or by medial vowel (e.g., *mit, pin, lick, fig, pill, lip, fin, rip*). Alternatively, they could simply not be organized by any particular feature other than the number of phonemes (e.g., miss, neck, sun, can, well, bet, man, pet). Four phonemes are more difficult, especially because they almost always include consonant blends (e.g., *black, first, slip, raft, pride*).

Some other materials might be helpful when you engage children in oral segmenting and blending. Picture cards can provide children with a concrete reference while they are working through a segmenting task. A puppet with a prominent mouth might be useful when you present segmented sounds that the children could then blend. A large rubber band or a slinky might be useful to remind the children that they are either stretching the sounds or combining them. None of these props is necessary, though, to begin using the strategy.

How Do You Prepare for Segmenting and Blending?

To prepare for segmenting and blending, you must first organize your word lists by relative difficulty. A useful tool for organizing word cards is a recipe box, with dividers labeled to indicate the various types of lists that you have prepared. In addition, you must be mindful of the purpose of this instruction—to teach children to do things that they cannot do on their own. Because of this, informal assessment is a necessary part of preparation. Remember that if a group of children can work with syllables, they need no more practice there—they should move immediately to onset–rime. Likewise, as soon as they can work with onset and rime, they should move to the phoneme. It is work at the level of the phoneme that is most complex and important, so it is important that children work at that level as quickly as possible.

How Do You Implement Segmenting and Blending?

Modeling is very important in segmenting and blending. First teach students to blend. As you work with sounds, some can be stretched easily and held, while others cannot; continuous sounds (e.g., /r/, /s/, /m/) should be elongated, while stop sounds (e.g., /b/, /p/, /d/) simply cannot be extended.

Model, using both kinds of sounds, and then have the students respond chorally: "I'll say the sounds in a word slowly, then you say them fast. ffff/iiii/zzzz. Say them fast. *Fizz*. mmmm/aaaa/nnnn. Say them fast. *Man*. p/iiii/nnnn. Say them fast. *Pin*."

Then teach children to segment the words, again, modeling first every day: "We're going to say the sounds in the word *fizz* slowly. /ffff/ /iiii/ /zzzz/. I hear three sounds in *fizz*. Let's say the sounds in *man*. /mmmm/ /aaaa/ /nnnn/. I hear three sounds in *man*. Say the sounds in *pin*. /p/ /iiii/ /nnnn/. I hear three sounds in *pin*."

You can choose to use a slinky to show that the sounds are stretched and then blended to make the procedure more concrete for the children.

How Do You Know If Segmenting and Blending Is Working?

You will know if this strategy is working when children can blend and segment a new word automatically. In order to spell new words, children must be able to segment them easily so that they can then match the sounds to letters; in order to read new words, they must be able to blend phonemes or onsets and rimes fluidly. Some assessments target these skills directly. In the previous chapter, we described phoneme segmentation assessments and also nonsense word decoding assessments that can provide more formal feedback about the efficacy of this strategy for individual children.

SAY-IT-AND-MOVE-IT

This strategy is slightly more complex than simple segmentation and blending, and we have seen it work well both for teachers and children. As with oral segmenting and blending, this strategy can be used with language units of increasing complexity—syllables, onsets and rimes, and finally phonemes. Unlike oral segmenting and blending, though, say-it-and-move-it requires manipulatives and can be used as a link between phonemic awareness and phonics.

What Kind of Reader Will Say-It-and-Move-It Help?

Say-it-and-move-it is so flexible that it can be used to differentiate for almost any kindergarten or first-grade reader. There are many ways to tell whether children would benefit from this strategy. A phoneme segmentation screening is one way, but so is a developmental spelling inventory or a nonsense word reading measure. In general, beginning readers who are working to develop automaticity at the one-syllable-word level benefit from say-it-and-move-it; it is up to you to plan to use say-it-and-move-it with sets of words that are appropriately difficult.

What Is the Instructional Focus for Say-It-and-Move-It?

When children say-it-and-move-it, they first segment and then blend. As with oral segmentation, you can match the unit (syllable, onset–rime, or phoneme) to the skills of a group of children. Initially, the technique provides simple, repetitive manipulation of objects to represent sounds. The tasks can progress from single-phoneme words to two-phoneme words, and then to three- and four-phoneme words. The teacher's role is to select the words, say them aloud, and monitor the students' manipulation of the objects as they first segment and then blend sounds.

Where Does Say-It-and-Move-It Come from?

Say-it-and-move-it is a version of a technique first developed by the Russian psychologist D. B. Elkonin. Elkonin proposed the use of sound boxes to help children conceptualize phonemes. Figure 3.4 provides an illustration of Elkonin boxes. For a group of children who are working on phoneme segmentation of three-phoneme words, each child is given a mat with three boxes and three manipulates. The teacher provides a word (e.g., *dog*) and children say each sound while moving a manipulative into a box. As they say the initial /d/, they move the first manipulative; as they say the medial vowel sound represented by the letter *o*, they move the second one, and as they say the final /g/, they move the final manipulative. Many researchers have used some form of Elkonin boxes in their work with beginning readers.

The label "say-it-and-move-it" was used by Ball and Blachman (1991) as part of an intervention for at-risk kindergarteners. They created a sequence of 44 lessons that were used with small groups of kindergarteners during their regular classroom literacy block (just as we are conceptualizing differentiated instruction) and, compared with controls, students in the intervention groups outperformed their peers on many different early literacy measures.

The lesson sequence for the intervention is available from Paul H. Brookes Publishing Co. (Blachman, Ball, Black, & Tangel, 2000), or it can be used as a more general differentiation strategy. In addition to the Elkonin boxes pictured in Figure 3.4, the intervention includes a simpler type of mat for children to use to manipulate sounds. It is a simple object with a line segment underneath, as in Fig-

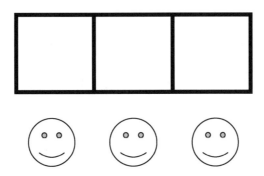

FIGURE 3.4. Elkonin boxes for teaching phoneme segmentation.

FIGURE 3.5. Say-it-and-move-it mat.

ure 3.5. Children are given manipulatives, as in the Elkonin procedure, and they are instructed to first keep them inside the object (in this case, the bicycle). Then they are given their word, and instructed to "say-it-and-move-it." At that time, they take their manipulatives and move them down, one at a time, to the line as they say the sounds. When they have finished segmenting, they blend the word back together.

What Materials Are Needed for Say-It-and-Move-It?

The basic materials for say-it-and-move-it are sound mats, manipulatives, and lists of words. The same advice for word lists you would use for oral segmenting and blending applies for say-it-and-move-it. Lists of words should be organized by difficulty of units (syllables, onset–rime, or phoneme) and by number of units (two-phoneme, three-phoneme). Figure 3.6 provides examples. One additional opportunity for say-it-and-move-it is to use letters (either plastic letters or letter tiles) to represent one or more of the phonemes (see Figure 3.7). For example, a group using this strategy to segment and blend the words *man*, *mat*, *mitt*, *mop*, and *men* could be provided with a plastic letter *m* and two disks. Likewise, a group working with *sit*, *tip*, *pin*, *lick*, *sip*, and *rip* could be provided with a plastic letter *i* and two disks.

Syllable practice		Onset–rime practice		Phoneme practice	
blackboard	table	map	bug	cot	him
shortstop	pencil	cap	dug	map	rag
keyboard	marker	sap	chug	hip	men
mailbox	staple	lap	hug	sit	win
backpack	crayon	tap	jug	pat	dot
airport	paper	nap	mug	bag	fun
slingshot	machine	rap		tan	fad
pigpen	copy	zap		rub	van
pitchfork	drawing			bed	set
trashcan	erase			wet	bat
Two-phoneme practice		Three-phoneme practice		Four-phoneme practice	
go	pay	bus	make	flap	fast
show	may	gas	kite	grass	risk
no	say	sack	hope	sleep	wink
row	we	sip	keep	skip	lamp
by	be	pen	fight	flip	sand
tie	she	net	time	snap	ramp
high	see	gum	take	step	help
sigh	key	web	same	drop	lost

FIGURE 3.6. Sample word lists for phonemic awareness activities.

From *Differentiated Reading Instruction* by Sharon Walpole and Michael C. McKenna. Copyright 2007 by The Guilford Press. Permission to photocopy this figure is granted to purchasers of this book for personal use only (see copyright page for details).

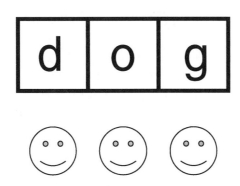

FIGURE 3.7. Elkonin boxes with letters.

How Do You Prepare for Say-It-and-Move-It?

There are two steps to prepare for say-it-and-move-it. First, you must gather materials—lists of words organized by difficulty with one, two, and three phonemes, Elkonin boxes or other sound mats, and manipulatives. One source to consider for selecting words is the phonics scope and sequence in the decoding portion of a core program. Manipulates might include buttons, bingo chips, or small plastic animals. One teacher we knew wanted to include letters, so she asked a local building supply company to donate a bucket of one-inch-square white bathroom tiles. She took some of the tiles and wrote letters on them, and left others blank (so that she could use them as manipulates representing sounds that the children did not yet connect with letters). That way she could give each child some blank tiles and some letter tiles, and since they were square, they worked nicely with her Elkonin boxes.

How Do You Implement Say-It-and-Move-It?

Once students know how to "say-it-and-move-it," they can do it easily without any procedural prompts. It makes sense, though, to teach the procedure directly at first. Ask students to line up their manipulatives (either under the Elkonin boxes or inside the shape on their sound mat) and to put the index finger of their dominant hand on one manipulative. Next, direct students to listen to each word, then stretch its sounds, moving one item for each sound.

Error correction strategies for teachers are important here. First, it may be necessary to do the same word several times, until the students can do it easily. If students struggle with the task, you can either model it on your own sound mat and have the child repeat, or actually move an individual child's finger while saying the sounds.

As students build letter-sound knowledge, you can make say-it-and-move-it more complex by using one letter or letter tile to indicate a target sound. For this to be reasonable, you must organize your word lists so that they have a common initial consonant sound, medial vowel sound, or final consonant sound.

How Do You Know If Say-It-and-Move-It Is Working?

Like our other phonemic awareness strategies, say-it-and-move-it can be evaluated during instruction. At first, if you have chosen an appropriate level of difficulty, children will find the tasks challenging. Gradually, however, as their segmentation skills increase, children will be able to segment virtually any word easily. That is a clear sign both that the strategy has worked and that it is no longer an important task during needs-based time.

TO LEARN MORE

Phonemic awareness is an important part of differentiated instruction in kindergarten and first grade. For well-written syntheses of research on phonemic awareness as a part of beginning reading, we recommend two texts: Marilyn Adams's (1990) *Beginning to Read: Thinking and Learning about Print* and Michael Pressley's (2006) *Reading Instruction That Works: The Case for Balanced Teaching, Third Edition.*

Excellent practical texts include Adams, Foorman, Lundberg, and Beeler's (1997) *Phonemic Awareness in Young Children: A Classroom Curriculum,* McGee and Morrow's (2005) *Teaching Literacy in Kindergarten,* and Ericson and Juliebö's (1998) *The Phonological Awareness Handbook for Kindergarten and Primary Teachers.*

CHAPTER 4

Building Word Recognition

The report of the NRP (National Institute of Child Health and Human Development, 2000) included a summary of experimental research (*www.nationalreading-panel.org/Publications/publications.htm*) on the effects of phonics instruction. As in the phonemic awareness chapter, the panel's charge involved combining the results of appropriate studies to identify findings that could be recommended with confidence. That report concluded that various types of systematic phonics instruction were effective in supporting reading, spelling, and comprehension, especially if they were provided during kindergarten and first grade.

RECENT RESEARCH AND REVIEWS

Since that time, there have been many studies published to further our understanding of the development of word recognition. Word recognition is the process by which readers match written representations of words with their sound and spelling in memory. None of these studies has contradicted the NRP findings, and some have extended them.

How do skilled readers learn words? The answer is not intuitive. Skilled readers read words by processing virtually every letter in every word (Adams, 1990). That means that they read words not by processing their configuration, or overall shape (processing each word as a whole, as if it were a picture), and not by relying on context clues to reduce their dependence on the letters—although both of those explanations "feel" right. In the area of word recognition, much of the important knowledge generated by laboratory studies contradicts what appears to be true when we read, because these cognitive processes are so automatic that they cannot be felt.

Young readers, children in their first years of school, cannot use these automatic processes in word recognition because they do not yet have the underlying alphabet knowledge. Linnea Ehri (1997) proposed that readers progress through phases of word learning. In the prealphabetic phase, children recognize words through environmental or visual cues that are not related to processing relationships between letters and sounds. For example, they might easily "read" names of products when they are presented within logos, or they might "read" the names of their classmates by remembering something about their visual configuration. Once children learn their letter names and sounds, they tend to recognize words by looking only at initial letters—a child named Keira might think that *kangaroo* and *kiss* are all *Kiera*. Ehri calls this partial alphabetic reading. When alphabet knowledge is more developed, children enter a full alphabetic phase. During this phase of word learning, they process each letter and sound in sequence, and they can "sound out" all regular consonant–vowel–consonant words. In the consolidated alphabetic phase, readers are not locked into sound-by-sound decoding; now they can process patterns. It is our goal to move all children to this phase by the end of first grade.

Some of our knowledge of word learning comes from investigations that are specifically designed to test theories rather than to teach reading directly. Roberts (2003) worked with preschool children (ages 3 and 4), most of whom were from families of low socioeconomic status and few of whom spoke English at home. She compared the effects of a small-group letter-name intervention, where children were taught letter names and shapes and basic rhyming strategies, with a comprehension intervention, where children engaged in explicit storybook reading, including fingerpoint reading. All of the children began the intervention with very weak letter-name knowledge. At the end of the intervention, the letter-name group scored higher on a special word-learning task that included letters they had learned. Children in the comprehension intervention scored higher on a word-learning task where words had visually distinct features. These findings indicate that even for very young children acquiring English, explicit instruction in letter names facilitates partial alphabetic reading, while comprehension–only interventions facilitate prealphabetic reading, a word recognition phase with very low utility. In other words, children learn to use what we teach them about word recognition; if we want them to use alphabetic strategies, we should begin teaching them immediately.

How should that initial knowledge be developed? The ideal scope and sequence of initial instruction in letter sounds still occasions debate, particularly among kindergarten teachers wedded to teaching one letter each week in the order of the alphabet. Experimental manipulations of all possible sequences of initial instruction are not reasonable. One way to design an order for instruction is to teach the most useful letters and letter patterns early so that readers might have more chances to use their letter-sound knowledge to read and spell words. Edward Fry

(2004) recently simplified an interesting analysis of the frequency of phoneme–grapheme relationships in a corpus of over 17,000 words. The basic question was this: How frequently are individual spelling patterns actually represented in English words? For vowels, the five most frequent phonemes in words were short *i* (in), short *a* (at), short *e* (end), the *r*-controlled sound (her), and long *o* (open). For consonant graphemes, the five most frequent were *r*, *t*, *n*, *s*, and *l*. Fry concluded by saying that frequency counts support the teaching of short vowel patterns before long, teaching the vowel–consonant–*e* pattern early in instruction, teaching long vowels in the open-syllable pattern, and teaching *r*-controlled vowels. He also specifically questioned the practice of teaching letter sounds in alphabetical order; frequency data simply do not support such a practice.

Williams and Hufnagel (2005) summarized the effects of a whole-group phonics and spelling approach on kindergarteners' spelling in their own journals. The instruction included letter sounds, letter patterns, high-frequency words, and strategies for reading and spelling unknown words. These words were displayed on a word wall so that children could use them easily to spell. Results indicated that the whole-group strategy was not equally effective for all children—the instruction was too easy for the highest-achieving children and too difficult for the lowest achievers. Only in the average-achieving group was transfer of the decoding instruction to the children's own writing noticeable. The authors concluded by suggesting that as early as the kindergarten year, teachers' use of groupings and differentiated, data-based instruction in decoding are necessary to serve the needs of all children.

White (2005) tested the effects of a systematic, explicit, *decoding-by-analogy* program on second-grade decoding and comprehension. Teachers taught a total of 200 words selected to represent all initial consonants, initial consonant blends and digraphs, and common vowel patterns. They also taught a series of high-frequency irregular words and multisyllabic words. All words were displayed on a word wall. Students were taught to use these words (either from memory or from the wall) to decode unknown words by analogy. This whole-class program increased decoding skills, but not reading comprehension.

One lingering (and important!) question related to word recognition is the issue of practice of phonics concepts in reading actual texts. Generally, many researchers (including us) recommend that teachers provide beginning readers with opportunities to read texts that include words with phonic elements that they have been learning. However, we do not find any basis in research for establishing specific percentages of decodable words for optimum decodability in beginning reading materials. Here is why we take that stance. Any time texts are manipulated to highlight word-level elements, they lose some of their integrity in terms of language and meaningfulness. The issue of decodability (which we define as the percentage of words that can be recognized based directly on previous instruction) is a hot-button issue in the design of instruction and intervention.

Research, including very recent research, is divided. Hiebert and Martin (2002) have recently considered the issue of the characteristics of texts for beginning readers. Individual sets of materials are typically categorized by their emphasis on high-frequency words, on decodable words, or on predictability; this is problematic because many texts contain a mix of these characteristics. In addition, research suggests that beginning readers find support in fluency from predictable books, but there is little evidence that this fluency transfers to word learning. Menon and Hiebert (2005) have proposed a radically new system, one that uses computers to level texts based on a complex formula for rating and relating multiple dimensions: high-frequency words, the number of instances of the same rime, word decodability (defined along a continuum), the number of distinct words, and supportiveness of text-level features. One study suggests that organizing and using a set of texts according to the formula has proven more effective in first-grade interventions than using literature-based basal materials (Menon & Hiebert, 2005).

In another study of texts for beginning readers, Jim Cunningham and his colleagues (Cunningham et al., 2005) investigated whether books leveled for the Reading Recovery intervention (which does not privilege decoding over context as a beginning word recognition strategy) would also be useful in interventions with a stronger emphasis on decoding. They found that the Reading Recovery texts did not provide extended opportunities for practice of decoding, particularly at the onset–rime level.

This issue is especially complicated given a recently reported intervention study comparing two first-grade interventions (Mathes, Denton, & Fletcher, 2005). One intervention drew heavily on concepts of direct instruction and used fully decodable texts. The other was more strategy oriented and used texts leveled for Reading Recovery. Combined with high-quality classroom instruction, both interventions were equally effective.

Given the complex and high-quality work of our colleagues, we cannot answer definitively what text characteristics are most important to give beginning readers practice in using their phonics knowledge. We continue to suspect that the match among reader and instruction and text is what is important; when choosing texts for practice of specific phonics concepts, they must be within the grasp of students in terms of language and level and they must allow for some opportunities for students to use their developing knowledge and skills to recognize new words.

FOUNDATIONAL TEACHER KNOWLEDGE

In 1999, Simmons and Kame'enui released curriculum maps to trace instructional goals in beginning reading (*reading.uoregon.edu/appendices/maps.php*). These maps included specific accomplishments in phonics and spelling across the elementary grades. Figure 4.1 lists them in the order in which they are first presented in the curriculum maps. Know, though, that many of these accomplishments are achieved at the same time by individual children (they are parallel rather than successive) and that others may take several months to actually master.

There are several issues in providing differentiated word recognition instruction. One is developing understanding of the scope and sequence of instruction, which will vary depending upon what materials are used. The second is the design of a system of assessment of children's specific knowledge of concepts previously taught, which requires teachers to choose and use phonics and spelling inventories. And the third issue is how to manage application of phonics concepts in reading and spelling words. Carol Tolman (2005) recently produced a table of basic phonics concepts that children are typically taught across the elementary years; it is adapted in Figure 4.2.

Children also need automatic word recognition for high-frequency words, some of which are phonetically irregular. Commercial reading programs include these words, generally in an order based both on frequency and on the texts that children are reading. In Figure 4.3, find a sample list of 300 words, organized by relative difficulty (Fry, 1980). These words must be recognized early and automatically because they form a high percentage of the total words in texts.

- Given a sound, can identify the letter.
- Given a letter, can produce a sound.
- Writes letters associated with sounds to spell words.
- Blends sounds to decode words.
- Reads common high-frequency words automatically.
- Given a letter combination, can produce a sound.
- Decodes consonant blends.
- Decodes common letter combinations.
- Reads regular one-syllable words.
- Spells regular one-syllable words conventionally.
- Spells all words with phonics-based strategies.
- Uses advanced phonic elements to recognize words.
- Decodes diphthongs and digraphs.
- Spells grade-level high-frequency words correctly.
- Reads compound words, contractions, possessives, inflectional endings.
- Reads multisyllabic words.
- Produces common word parts.
- Uses word meaning and word order to confirm decoding efforts.
- Spells contractions, possessives, inflectional endings.

FIGURE 4.1. Development of phonics skills as presented in Simmons and Kame'enui's (1999) curriculum maps for kindergarten and first grade.

Phonics instructional goals	
Letter names	In order of utility
Consonant sounds	In order of utility
Consonant blends	*st-, sm-, sn-, qu-, sl-, sp-, sc-, sk-, bl-, cl-, fl-, gl-, pl-, br-, cr-, dr-, fr-, gr-, pr-, tr-, sw-, tw-, spr-, str-, scr-, spl-, mp, nd, sk, st, ft, lk, ld*
Digraphs and trigraphs	*sh, ch, ng, ph, th, wh, tch, dge*
Silent letter patterns	*kn, mb, gn, mn, pn*
Orthographic patterns	*-ck, -ff, -ss, -ll, -zz*
Vowel sounds	Short and long, represented by single letter
Vowel teams	*ai, ay, ei, eigh, ey, ie, ee, ei, ie, igh, ie, oe, oa, ow, oo, ew, ue*
Diphthongs	*oi, oy, ou, ow*
R-controlled vowels	*er, ir, ur, or, ar*
Syllable types	Closed, vowel–consonant–e, open, vowel team, consonant-*le*, *r*-controlled
Morphemes	Prefixes, suffixes

FIGURE 4.2. Basic phonics concepts for children to master. Adapted from Tolman (2005). Copyright 2005 by the International Dyslexia Association. Adapted by permission of Carol Tolman.

Decoding-by-analogy programs after first grade rely on a list of words to represent high-frequency spelling patterns, but they are organized and selected for different reasons. Figure 4.4 includes a list of 200 words used in a recent study of analogy-based decoding instruction in second grade (White, 2005). Similar lists could be generated to support third-grade decoding in needs-based groups by combining the scope and sequence of phonics instruction for first and second grades in a core program.

Developing specific phonics concepts is necessary but not sufficient for developing automatic word recognition; in fact, the goal of phonics instruction is to develop such a large, fully automatic reading vocabulary that consciously applied phonics-based strategies for word recognition are only very rarely needed. During the period of reading acquisition, however, supporting novice readers in applying phonics strategies when they encounter unknown words is one of the keys to developing automaticity and independence. Such support during reading, often called coaching, is much easier said than done; to be effective, teacher coaching must be immediate, understandable to the child, and successful in promoting decoding. Coaching must replace the strategy of simply giving the unknown word or

the	but	some	long	good	put	off	school	always	stop
of	not	her	down	sentence	end	play	father	those	without
and	what	would	day	man	does	spell	keep	both	second
a	all	make	did	think	another	air	tree	paper	late
to	were	like	get	say	well	away	never	together	miss
in	we	him	come	great	large	animal	start	got	idea
is	when	into	made	where	must	house	city	group	enough
you	your	time	may	help	big	point	earth	often	eat
that	can	has	part	through	even	page	eye	run	face
it	said	look	over	much	such	letter	light	important	watch
he	there	to	new	before	because	mother	thought	until	far
was	use	more	sound	line	turn	answer	head	children	Indian
for	an	right	take	right	here	found	under	side	real
on	each	go	only	too	why	study	story	feet	almost
are	which	see	little	mean	ask	still	saw	car	let
as	she	number	work	old	went	learn	left	mile	above
with	do	no	know	any	men	should	don't	night	girl
his	how	way	place	same	read	America	few	walk	sometimes
they	their	could	year	tell	need	world	while	while	mountain
I	if	people	live	boy	land	high	along	sea	cut
at	will	my	me	follow	different	every	might	began	young
be	up	than	back	came	home	near	close	grow	talk
this	other	first	give	went	us	add	something	took	soon
have	about	water	most	show	move	food	seem	river	list
from	out	been	very	also	try	between	next	for	song
or	many	call	after	around	kind	own	hard	carry	leave
one	then	who	thing	form	hand	below	open	state	family
had	them	oil	hour	tree	picture	country	example	once	body
by	these	now	just	small	again	plant	begin	book	music
word	so	find	name	set	change	last	life	hear	color

FIGURE 4.3. High-frequency word list, organized top to bottom and left to right. Adapted from Fry (1980). Copyright 1980 by the International Reading Association. Adapted by permission.

a	broke	discover	fun	his	map	place	slide	these	water
about	bug	do	get	horn	me	plane	smart	they	way
after	but	does	girl	how	more	president	smile	thing	we
all	by	down	five	hurt	music	price	snake	think	went
am	can	dragon	glad	I	my	question	some	this	were
an	car	dream	glove	if	name	rain	sound	those	what
and	careful	end	go	in	no	red	spider	time	when
animals	champ	excitement	good	is	noise	right	splash	to	where
are	city	fell	grab	it	not	run	spring	too	which
ask	clock	find	green	job	now	said	stop	treat	who
at	club	fine	grew	jump	of	saw	street	truck	will
back	coat	fish	gym	kick	off	scary	swim	two	with
be	come	five	had	know	old	school	talk	unhappy	work
because	could	flag	happy	let	on	see	teacher	up	would
best	creature	fly	has	like	one	shark	that	us	write
big	cricket	food	have	look	or	she	the	use	year
bleed	dance	for	he	long	out	ship	their	vacation	yes
blue	Dave	friend	her	made	over	show	them	very	you
boy	day	frog	here	make	people	skate	then	want	your
brave	did	from	him	many	phone	sleep	there	was	zoo

FIGURE 4.4. Words used to teach decoding by analogy. Adapted from White (2005). Copyright 2005 by the International Reading Association. Adapted by permission.

of moving attention away from the word and into semantic connections. Coaching is so highly individualized that it can only be used during needs-based small groups as students are reading texts that allow them to integrate their automatic word recognition skills and their phonetic analysis skills in real text. Kathleen Clark (2004) has studied teachers' talk during such small-group reading activities. She produced very useful examples of teacher talk as teachers coached word recognition. She has also couched her description of coaching of word recognition with reference to stages of word learning. She cautions teachers to choose cues for children who are learning to decode so as to direct children's attention to fully analyzing sound and spelling patterns in words and to use syntactic cues to check whether decoding efforts have been successful. Figure 4.5 summarizes her work.

In the remaining sections in this chapter, we present strategies for applying research in word recognition to support children's decoding growth. Each is designed to be sensitive to children's development of word recognition strategies and also to specific phonics units that are to be taught and learned.

General cues to prompt thought	
Questions	Statements
What do you know/think about that? What are you going to do to help yourself out? If you're stuck, what can you do? How are you going to figure that out?	Look for something you already know how to do. Look and think what you need to do.

Cues to prompt specific action		
Using specific letter sounds	Using word-part strategies	Using context to check decoding
The first *g* is hard. Throw away the *gh*. The *y* is acting like an *i*. It's a blend.	Is there a part you know? Look for a little word. Can you take something off?	This is what you said. Does that make sense? Does that sound right?

FIGURE 4.5. Teacher strategies for coaching word recognition. Adapted from Clark (2004). Copyright 2004 by the International Reading Association. Adapted by permission.

TEACHING LETTER NAMES AND SOUNDS

All types of phonics instruction *and* effective word recognition strategies both depend upon thorough grounding in the alphabet. In fact, the general concept that specific letters in the English alphabet are used to represent specific sounds in the English language, the alphabetic principle, comes as children learn the fairly abstract concept of specific letter-name–letter-sound correspondences. The goal with letters and sounds is to reach automaticity so that a reader does not have to expend any cognitive energy trying to remember a specific sound and can use attention instead to blend sounds or to recognize more complex spelling patterns. On the way to learning the letter sounds automatically, children usually learn to sing the alphabet, to say the alphabet, and to track the alphabet while they say it. For some children, automatic access to an individual letter name or sound does not easily follow that initial progression.

What Kind of Reader Will Letter-Name and Letter-Sound Instruction Help?

Kindergarten readers who are not learning their letter names and sounds through whole-class activities may need additional instruction in needs-based groups. These readers will score poorly on measures of letter-name fluency and also on informal letter-name and letter-sound inventories, in which all letters are displayed in random order. This instructional strategy is meant for children who can sing, say, and track the alphabet, but cannot reliably produce letter names and sounds in isolation.

What Is the Instructional Focus of Letter-Name and Letter-Sound Instruction?

The instructional focus for letter-name and letter-sound instruction is on children recognizing that a particular pattern of straight lines, slanted lines, and curves is reliably associated with a specific name and with at least one common sound. Children must master this association for both upper-case and lower-case letters.

Where Does Letter-Name and Letter-Sound Instruction Come from?

We know of no specific study to credit for this strategy; rather it is a common feature of all instruction and intervention programs to move emergent readers to beginning reading. The general instructional strategy that we are using is called distributed practice—a very brief repetitive practice every day.

What Materials Are Needed for Letter-Name and Letter-Sound Instruction?

To teach children to recognize and remember letter names and sounds, teachers need letters! There are many forms to keep the instruction interesting (letter cards and tiles, magnetic letters, foam letters) and many ways to organize sets of letters (plastic bags, buckets, pocket charts) for teacher modeling. The key to using this procedure is to decide the order in which you will teach the letters and to organize your materials so that you can do so without additional preparation

Many core reading programs come with a set of alphabet letters with cue words to help children remember the most common sound of each letter. Generally, those materials are displayed above the blackboard, and the teacher refers to them with a pointer during whole-group instruction. Bringing the letters and their sound cues down closer to the children is useful for those who are struggling, as is the use of alphabet strips and personal tagboard cards that contain the letters and the cues. Many core program materials include sets of reproducible alphabet cards; we encourage teachers to duplicate them and to use them in needs-based instruction so that the cues that children are learning during whole-class instruction are the same ones that they are reviewing in needs-based instruction.

We also encourage you to use paper and pencil or dry erase boards and markers during needs-based instruction. Letter recognition is aided by close attention to the patterns used to form letters—handwriting procedures, if matched to the scope and sequence of letter-name instruction, can be very helpful here. In addition, fluid formation of letters encourages children to participate in invented spelling exercises, developing their phonemic awareness and applying their phonics knowledge.

How Do You Prepare for Letter-Name and Letter-Sound Instruction?

Preparing for letter-name and letter-sound instruction includes two basic steps. First, decide on a scope and sequence for instruction (most often the one in the core reading program) and organize your letter manipulatives for easy access. Next, use a phonics inventory to find out which of the letters already taught are still unknown to any one of the students in the group. Those letters can then be organized into sets of four. With respect to pacing, teach each set of four letters for three days, and then review all previously taught letters.

How Do You Implement Letter-Name and Letter-Sound Instruction?

When you are working with a new letter, we urge you to be very explicit about it. Many teachers begin lessons by asking the students, "Who knows what letter this is?" In a needs-based group, though, teachers already know that the students do not know the letter, so engaging in this type of guessing game is unwise and it wastes precious small-group time. Rather than have the students guess, be direct. "The name of this letter is ____. What name?" (Students respond chorally.) "The sound of this letter is ____. What sound?" (Students respond chorally.) For new letters, some additional instruction might be useful. "Here is a new letter. Watch me write it." The teacher demonstrates, verbalizing the strokes. "Now you write it with me" (in the air or on dry-erase boards). "The name of this letter is ____. What name?" (Students respond chorally.) "The sound of this letter is ____. What sound?" (Students respond chorally.) Once all of the day's letters are introduced, teachers can repeatedly and rapidly ask students to identify the letters or produce the sounds. After the introduction, 3 to 5 minutes of work in the small group would constitute efficient distributed practice.

How Do You Know If Letter-Name and Letter-Sound Instruction Is Working?

Continuous assessment of letter-name and letter-sound knowledge is both easy and essential. A letter-name or letter-sound inventory can be administered every 2 or 3 weeks to determine which letters students have learned and which they still do not know. In addition, each day the teacher can easily assess one child in the small group, simply by asking him or her to produce the letter names and sounds. By the end of the week, each of five students could be assessed in this way.

TEACHING SOUNDING AND BLENDING

Letter-name and letter-sound knowledge, in and of itself, is useless. In order to use that knowledge, teachers must engage students in active recognition of real words. We call sound-by-sound decoding "sounding it out," where students recognize an unknown word by producing individual letter sounds and then combining them, or sounding and blending.

What Kind of Reader Will Sounding and Blending Help?

We favor this use of sounding and blending as the first word recognition strategy. For children with "average" development, this might be appropriate for the middle of kindergarten. Struggling students might need differentiated work on sounding and blending through the first grade. Sound and blending success depends on mastery of letter sounds, at least for the ones that are in the target words.

Teaching sounding and blending skills directly will help children who do not choose to use phonics knowledge to recognize unknown words. Such children will score poorly on nonsense word decoding tasks and probably on real-word decoding tasks as well. They will also score poorly on developmental spelling tasks, which ask children to use their word knowledge to spell words that they have not memorized or practiced. Sounding and blending strategies are particularly appropriate for children who know their letter names and have at least some knowledge of letter sounds.

What Is the Instructional Focus of Sounding and Blending?

The focus of sounding and blending is recognizing graphemes, producing associated phonemes, and blending the sounds to make words. The emphasis in on strategic use of letter sounds, and instruction is meant to guide students to use letter-sound knowledge when they come to an unknown word during reading. It is also geared only for recognition of words that are already part of an individual's meaning vocabulary—words that are part of the reader's own oral vocabulary, but not yet in his or her store of sight words.

Where Does Sounding and Blending Come from?

Sounding and blending is part of all phonics programs. In fact, sounding and blending strategies are even used in programs where the unit of instruction is larger than the phoneme. Such programs might have children sound an onset and then a rime, and blend those two units (e.g., /p/ /in/ *pin*). The difference is that the vowel is never sounded alone, but the procedure for recognizing words is the same as in sound-by-sound programs. In research, sounding-and-blending approaches are sometimes referred to as "direct code" instruction or as "direct instruction" in decoding.

What Materials Are Needed for Sounding and Blending?

As in all strategies for building word recognition, the most essential materials to assemble are words! Selection of which words to use, though, is not a trivial matter. In truly differentiated instruction, the words that are selected for focus must actually represent a unique corpus—words that students have the underlying letter-sound knowledge to recognize, but ones that they have not yet established as personal sight words. If a student can recognize a word by sight, it is senseless to ask him or her to sound and blend it.

As in most small-group work, it is useful to have a large-sized set of manipulatives for modeling. These might be simple index cards with words printed on them, and a pocket chart to manage them. Personal sets of word cards are useful so that students can practice and receive feedback after the modeling. Finally, dry-erase boards are useful for assessing deep understanding of the target words; if students have sounded and blended an individual word successfully and repeatedly, they can often spell it easily. At the very least, after sounding and blending practice, the students should be able to listen to a word presented orally, segment its sounds, match them to letters, and write them.

One final category of materials that might be useful in sounding and blending is a set of simple little books that contain words that match the scope and sequence of the students' phonics instruction. This option is likely to be viable only if the books either are specifically designed to highlight a particular feature that students are learning (e.g., short *a* patterns) or are developed by the authors of the core series and provide cumulative review. One thing that we caution against is providing differentiated sounding and blending instruction with words in isolation and then giving children random leveled books that are independent of such instruction; the likely message to children when providing only isolated sounding and blending is confusing, because word recognition in isolation and word recognition in text are not connected. When there are at least some words in the text that have the same feature that children are learning as they work with words in isolation, teachers communicate to children that they can use sounding and blending techniques in real reading.

How Do You Prepare for Sounding and Blending?

The key to differentiated sounding and blending instruction (and the key difference between such instruction and simple small-group instruction) is that the instruction is actually planned to address a need that the students demonstrate. If possible, use a phonics inventory or a spelling inventory to determine what phonics knowledge students are lacking. We have worked with teachers who, at first, are overwhelmed by the idea that their students are not developing decoding skills at all. Then, after collecting data to see what they do know, the teachers realize that there are specific areas with which specific students need help. After initial instruction, phonics knowledge is rarely an all-or-nothing proposition.

Once you know where to start instruction, it is much easier to prepare a series of lessons at once rather than one at a time. The key component is a readily available list of words that share common phonics elements or patterns. Like most aspects of needs-based instruction, once these words are chosen, they can be used for different groups of children at different times or in different years. It makes good sense to prepare carefully the first time and to organize materials for easy access.

One strategy for preparing for sounding and blending instruction is to use the scope and sequence in the core phonics program as a guide. Compare results for the weakest child in the group with the scope and sequence for instruction in phonics. Begin reteaching at that point, simply using the repetitive strategy of sounding and blending with specific words (or new words with the same phonic elements) that have been previously taught during whole-group phonics instruction. An added benefit of that strategy for preparing is that many of the word cards will already be included in the classroom materials. Alternatively, the scope and sequence can provide a general guide for the order in which phonic elements could be introduced, and you can use additional exemplars of the patterns.

How Do You Implement Sounding and Blending?

The key to making any instructional strategy work is to tell what the strategy is, how to use it, and when and why it would be helpful. Although the words that provide the meat of each lesson might be different every day, your teacher talk can be the same: "We are going to start today by sounding and blending some words. The way that you do that is to look at each letter, say each sound out loud, and then say them fast to make a word. Listen to me. /p/ /i/ /g/ *pig*. Now you try: /p/ /i/ /g/ *pig*. When you come to a word that you don't know you can sound and blend it."

Sounding and blending can also be used as children begin to learn vowel patterns. The teacher language would be the same with this modification: "Say the first sound and then say the vowel pattern and then say them fast to make a word. Listen to me. /p/ /ig/ *pig*. Now you try."

How Do You Know If Sounding and Blending Is Working?

You will know that sounding and blending instruction is working when children can sound and blend novel words without support. Remember that the target of sounding and blending is first to teach a strategy that children can employ when they encounter novel words and second to build automatic recognition of the words used in instruction. After instruction in short *a* across many vowel patterns, children should be able to sound and blend any three-phoneme short *a* word. Another way to assess the efficacy of this strategy is through a nonsense word decoding task; children who can decode nonsense words can do so only by using letter-sound knowledge. Unlike real words, some of which are simply known to individual children because of their reading experience, nonsense words are true tests of the application of phonics knowledge.

TEACHING LETTER PATTERNS

Although sounding and blending strategies can be used either for sound-by-sound decoding or in short-vowel word-family work, we have chosen another strategy that is specifically targeted at units of the spelling system that are larger than the phoneme. Teaching children letter patterns (rather than simply letter sounds) allows them to recognize words with similar patterns more quickly than they could by using sounding and blending of individual sounds. In fact, Wylie and Durrell (1970) identified 37 high-frequency patterns with which children could recognize over 500 words. Their list is included in Figure 4.6.

What Kind of Reader Will Teaching Letter Patterns Help?

Teaching letter patterns, particularly high-frequency short-vowel patterns, is a useful strategy for beginning readers who know their letter sounds and can sound and blend but have not yet attained automaticity. Teaching children to blend onsets to vowel patterns demands that they hold fewer items in short-term memory as they decode unknown words.

What Is the Instructional Focus of Teaching Letter Patterns?

The focus of this strategy is development of automatic recognition of high-frequency vowel patterns (e.g., -at, -an, -ag, -ad, -ap, -ip, -ig, -in, -ill) so that children can recognize them when combined with any onset at the word level. This strategy teaches children to sound and blend, but not at the individual sound level.

ack	at	ight	op
ail	ate	ill	ore
ain	aw	in	ot
ake	ay	ine	uck
ale	eat	ing	ug
ame	ell	ink	ump
an	est	ip	unk
ank	ice	it	
ap	ide	ock	
ash	ick	oke	

FIGURE 4.6. High-frequency vowel patterns. Based on Wylie and Durrell (1970).

Where Does Teaching Letter Patterns Come from?

This strategy is used in many, many beginning reading programs and interventions; we cannot identify its origin. However, an especially useful text for preparing and implementing the strategy is Bear et al.'s (2004) *Words Their Way: Word Study for Phonics, Vocabulary, and Spelling Instruction*. This text details a scope and sequence and many instructional strategies that together constitute word study—an approach to developing word knowledge through increasingly complex tiers of sound, spelling, and meaning. Variations on this approach have been used in successful tutoring and intervention programs (Invernizzi, Rosemary, Juel, & Richards, 1997; Morris, Shaw, & Perney, 1990).

The key to teaching vowel patterns is to contrast two or three patterns in a procedure called word sorting. Word sorting involves layers of categorization—simply taking a group of words and separating them into piles with like features. Words can be sorted by their initial sound (as in the initial-sound picture sorting we described earlier), by their ending sound (as in a sort of *-an*, *-ap*, and *-at* words), or by their medial vowel sound (as in a sort of *-en*, *-in*, and *-an* words). Beginning consonant sorts are easiest, ending sound sorts are more difficult, and medial vowel sorts are most difficult.

What Materials Are Needed for Teaching Letter Patterns?

As in all of our strategies for differentiation the key materials are words, preferably presented on word cards. The ideal is a large set for modeling and small sets for individual students in the group. For this strategy to work, the words must be organized around their vowel patterns. For example, teachers must have many specific lists of eight to ten words that constitute the patterns to be mastered.

How Do You Prepare for Teaching Letter Patterns?

The key to preparing to teach letter patterns is to identify the patterns to be taught and then break them into logical groups. One strategy is to research the scope and sequence of phonics instruction in the core reading program and organize the patterns that way. In initial lessons, as students are learning the sorting strategy, contrast just two families. When students understand the procedure, move to three families. Plan to work with the same sets of words for 3 days, and then review.

As with the other strategies for developing word recognition, not all letter patterns need to be taught during needs-based instruction. Assessments, particularly phonics or spelling assessments, can help you identify patterns that children need to learn. The authors of *Words Their Way* argue that new patterns should be combined with known ones. For example, if children are struggling with short *e* patterns (e.g., -et, -en) it might be useful to teach them together with some patterns that they do know (e.g., -at, -an).

How Do You Implement Teaching Letter Patterns?

At the beginning of each lesson, use direct explanation to teach the patterns: "Today we will work on reading and spelling three vowel patterns. The /at/ pattern is the sound at the end of the word *cat*. It is spelled *a-t*. The /et/ pattern is the sound at the end of the word *pet*. It is spelled *e-t*. The /it/ pattern is the sound at the end of the word *sit*. It is spelled *i-t*. First I want you to listen to words and tell me whether they sound like *cat*, *pet*, or *sit*." At this point, pronounce five or six words to represent each pattern, and ask the children to group words with like sounds together. Next, highlight the spelling patterns again. "Let's look at the spellings for all of the words that sound like *cat*. Notice that words with the /at/ sound have the *a-t* pattern. You can use that pattern when you read or spell *a-t* words."

After you have introduced and modeled the sorting of the day's words, children can read, sort, and even spell their own sets of words. During that time, continue to model the strategy if necessary and to provide corrective feedback as children work with the pattern; in fact, if no corrective feedback is necessary, that is a good sign that the patterns chosen for the day are not challenging enough to constitute differentiated instruction.

How Do You Know If Teaching Letter Patterns Is Working?

During vowel letter-pattern instruction, you will have ample opportunities to watch children work with the day's words. It is important to notice whether children are actually able to read and spell the specific words chosen to represent the day's patterns. However, that is not enough. You will know that this strategy is working when children can read and spell novel words containing taught patterns, and when they can transfer their knowledge of patterns to nearly automatic decoding of words in isolation and in context. Such transfer of skills from one word to another constitutes development of deep word knowledge rather than development of surface knowledge of individual words.

TEACHING IRREGULAR HIGH-FREQUENCY WORDS

Many words that children must read automatically in text are not easily taught in a scope and sequence of sounding and blending or of letter patterns. Consider the first column of words in Figure 4.3—*from*, *one*, and *have*, for example, have irregular spellings. However, these particular words are so common in text that children simply must learn them early and well.

What Kind of Reader Will Teaching High-Frequency Words Help?

All readers need to add to their store of automatically recognized high-frequency words as they move across the elementary grades. Some readers, however, need more work, either with those words whose orthographic features are not entirely consistent with their phonological features (e.g., *of*), or with those words whose orthographic features are generally too complex (e.g., *eight*) at the time they must be learned. A reader who struggles with high-frequency words may do well on a phonics survey or on a nonsense word decoding task and still have low scores in rate and accuracy in oral reading fluency measures. Sometimes the cause of such a profile is a lack of automaticity with the high-frequency words rather than a lack of decoding skills and strategies.

What Is the Instructional Focus of Teaching High-Frequency Words?

The focus of high-frequency word lessons is on making explicit ties between the spoken and written forms of particular words. A high-frequency word inventory, spelling or writing samples, or oral reading errors can reveal specific words that can be taught using this strategy, or teachers can use this strategy to teach or review the core high-frequency words for the current or previous grade level.

Where Does Teaching High-Frequency Words Come from?

This technique for teaching high frequency words is an adaptation of the strategy for fully analyzing words that was developed by Irene Gaskins and Linnea Ehri for the Benchmark School (Gaskins, Ehri, & Cress, 1996). At Benchmark, a private school for dyslexic children outside Philadelphia, this basic procedure is used to teach many words, including phonetically regular ones, in a specific word identification program. The reason that we have adopted this procedure specifically for differentiated instruction of high-frequency words is that we have watched many teachers teach children to memorize high-frequency words through rote repetition rather than to understand how the spellings of these words work.

What Materials Are Needed for Teaching High-Frequency Words?

The only materials that are needed to teach high-frequency words are words and Elkonin boxes (refer to Figure 3.4). This time, though, the boxes could be much longer. For example, the word *because* has five sounds: /b/ /e/ /k/ /u/ /z/. A five-compartment box would be needed to teach that word. In fact, it might be most efficient to simply photocopy a grid with many rows of boxes.

How Do You Prepare for Teaching High-Frequency Words?

The first step in preparing to teach high-frequency words is to locate them. You could find many websites that list high-frequency words, or you could use the list we have provided. However, such an approach constitutes random attention to developing word knowledge; the words that are taught may or may not appear in the texts that children are reading. A more integrated approach (at least for teachers using a basal reading program) would be to generate a list of high-frequency words in order of presentation from the core scope and sequence. That list could be used as a screening tool—that is, you could simply ask children to read the words, and note the ones that students do not know. Small sets of words (three to five) could be taught each day, with periodic review of previously taught words.

How Do You Implement Teaching High-Frequency Words?

Again, we envision this instruction to take fewer than 5 minutes of instructional time. Begin by using direct explanation and modeling for each word: "Today we are going to learn to read and spell some really useful words: The first word is *from*. Say that word. Now watch me count the sounds in *from*. /f/ /r/ /u/ /m/. We hear four sounds. Say the sounds with me. Now watch me spell the word *from*. The first sound we hear in *from* is /f/, and it is spelled with the letter *f*. The second sound we hear in from is /r/, and it is spelled with the letter *r*. The third sound we hear in *from* is /u/, and it is spelled with the letter *o*. The last sound we hear in *from* is /m/, and it is spelled with the letter *m*. Three of the letters and sounds in *from* are easy to remember. The only one that is tricky is the *o*. Remember that in the word *from*, the /u/ sound is spelled with the letter *o*. If you remember that, you can easily read and spell *from*."

The key to teaching high-frequency words is to explain the relationship between graphemes and phonemes in the word, drawing attention to which are familiar and which need more attention. The insight that it is not the whole word that is tricky, but rather one sound or pattern, is the key to unlocking the word and simplifying the memory task for a beginning reader.

How Do You Know If Teaching High-Frequency Words Is Working?

You will know it is working if children begin to read and spell taught words more automatically. You can give a cumulative spelling test every 2 weeks to monitor progress—spelling tests can be given to the entire group at once. Remember that decoding is easier than spelling; students who can spell the words accurately can also read the words accurately; students who cannot spell them may be able to read them, but further instruction is necessary.

TEACHING DECODING BY ANALOGY

A final strategy for developing word knowledge is teaching decoding by analogy. Decoding by analogy is cognitively challenging and demands the most careful planning of the strategies we have summarized here. The benefit of such planning is that decoding by analogy, as presented in the strategy we describe here, can be transferred from single-syllable words to multisyllabic words—the stumbling block for many struggling readers after they have mastered decoding of first-grade words and texts.

What Kind of Reader Will Decoding by Analogy Help?

Readers who have mastered sounding and blending strategies and have learned many vowel letter patterns in individual words but cannot apply them in recognizing new words may benefit from decoding by analogy. Such readers may score well on single-syllable phonics or spelling inventories but struggle to read and spell multisyllabic words. Decoding by analogy can be used for readers in second and third grades, and also for struggling older readers.

What Is the Instructional Focus of Decoding by Analogy?

Decoding by analogy requires students to learn a corpus of words chosen to represent high-frequency spelling patterns, to identify the spelling patterns within those target words, and to use those words to unlock sound and spellings of unknown words.

Where Does Decoding by Analogy Come from?

Many decoding programs after grade 1 rely partly on decoding by analogy. We adapt this strategy from the research conducted at The Benchmark School and from a recent research study (Gaskins, 1999; White, 2005). Figure 4.4 lists the words used as anchor words to teach decoding by analogy to second graders in White's (2005) study. Specific information about Benchmark's program, including information about training in decoding by analogy, is available on the school's website (*www.benchmarkschool.org/*).

What Materials Are Needed for Decoding by Analogy?

The key materials for decoding by analogy are the clue words representing high-frequency spelling patterns. This list could be generated from the scope and sequence of phonics instruction for the first and second grades combined. These can be displayed on a class word wall or a personal chart.

How Do You Prepare for Decoding by Analogy?

Decoding by analogy is a highly specialized, cognitively demanding strategy for word recognition. The first step in preparation for teaching decoding by analogy is to internalize a script. Teachers need to be able to verbalize the strategy clearly: "When I don't know a word, I look for the first spelling pattern (the vowel and what comes after). I think about my clue words and find a word with the same pattern. (The clue word might be located on the word wall under the vowel letter.) I tell myself that if I know this clue word, the new word must sound like it. Then I look for the next spelling pattern. When I've come to the end, I blend the syllables together and check to see that my word makes sense."

How Do You Implement Decoding by Analogy?

The first step to implementing decoding by analogy is to make sure that children can read and analyze the set of clue words. The clue words must represent all of the vowel patterns that the children are to use to decode new words. Next you must be willing to model the decoding of new words by analogy to these known words. For example, you might teach the word *frightening* because it was coming up in a story that the children would be reading. Use the analogy script: "I don't know this word. I see the spelling pattern *i-g-h*. I think of a word I know with the same pattern. It might be on the wall. If I know *night*, this part must be *fright*. The next pattern that I see is *e-n*. If I know *pen*, this must be *ten. Fright-ten. Frighten.*"

Once teachers have taught the clue words and modeled the use of the clue words to decode unknown words, the real work of decoding by analogy begins. During oral reading, prompt students to verbalize decoding-by-analogy procedures as they tackle unknown words. Such coaching during word recognition is very challenging teaching, but it is essential in moving struggling decoders to more complex words.

How Do You Know If Decoding by Analogy Is Working?

This strategy can be monitored by students' willingness to try it on their own and by their success in doing so. First, they must be able to describe the procedures involved in the strategy. Then they must actually remember to use the strategy during reading. You know that this strategy is working when students can quickly verbalize the script and begin to use it on their own, without prompting.

TO LEARN MORE

We realize that differentiating word recognition instruction is a daunting task and that we have not provided sufficient guidance to answer all questions that teachers may have about it. Our general advice, though, is this: Start using these very simple strategies to begin to differentiate while you continue to build your knowledge. In our experience, teachers rarely differentiate their word recognition instruction by providing direct instruction with words in isolation; rather, they tend to rely on opportune moments to "coach" students to recognize words during fluency work. Reliance on teachable moments, however, is not likely to be effective with struggling readers. It is simply not systematic and intensive enough to give struggling readers the boost they need.

We have given you a start with some simple strategies that you can apply right away. You may want to read more about phonics and spelling instruction. A quite comprehensive description of the underlying language systems (sound, spelling, syntax, and meaning) is presented in *Speech to Print: Language Essentials for Teachers* (Moats, 2000). Fox's (2005) *Phonics for the Teacher of Reading* and Cunningham's (2005) *Phonics They Use: Words for Reading and Writing* provide simpler, but useful reviews of phonics generalizations. Ganske's (2000) *Word Journeys* and Bear et al.'s (2004) *Words Their Way: Word Study for Phonics, Vocabulary, and Spelling Instruction* each provide very useful developmental spelling inventories to help teachers focus and direct their differentiated time as well as words and procedures that you could use in differentiated, needs-based small groups. *Success with Struggling Readers: The Benchmark School Approach* (Gaskins, 2005) will help you to understand more about decoding by analogy. Developing word knowledge in children requires you to continue to learn about words and how they work.

CHAPTER 5

Building Fluency

In Chapters 3 and 4, we have described instructional strategies teachers can use to develop two of the basic proficiencies—phonemic awareness and word recognition—that underlie skilled reading. Often, those skills are tested on measures that have *fluency* in their titles (e.g., letter-name or phoneme-segmentation fluency). We prefer to call rapid performance in these lower-level processes automaticity in order to distinguish these processes from reading fluency. Automaticity in basic skills, particularly in word recognition, is a requirement for true reading fluency, but it is not the same thing. Reading fluency, the ability to read with appropriate rate, accuracy, and prosody, is a different part of the differentiation puzzle, one that has enjoyed increasing attention. In this chapter, we describe instructional strategies for differentiated support of reading fluency.

The NRP's (National Institute of Child Health and Human Development, 2000) research synthesis (*www.nationalreadingpanel.org/Publications/publications. htm*) included a chapter on the development of fluency in classrooms. That report concluded that guided oral reading was a powerful fluency practice. Unfortunately, the panel could not locate convincing evidence that the most common and popular approach to increasing reading fluency—wide self-selected reading—built fluency. Negative reaction to this finding was widespread; it defies conventional wisdom. However, the NRP was not charged with producing a summary of conventional wisdom; they were to locate and summarize evidence drawn from experimental studies. Under that constraint, they were unable to document a convincing relationship between self-selected reading and fluency growth.

RECENT RESEARCH AND REVIEWS

A powerful and positive result of the NRP report has been additional studies and research reviews. Since the panel's report, researchers have continued to consider the issue of fluency development in classrooms. In 2002, Chard, Vaughn, and Tyler published a synthesis of research on building reading fluency in elementary-school students with learning disabilities (LDs). They examined the results of 24 studies. All of them included some form of repeated reading. Like the NRP, they found support for the use of oral reading during instruction. They also found that interventions that include modeling fluent reading had stronger effects than those where students simply read and reread on their own. The most powerful interventions used the teacher as model, but interventions where students used computer-based or audiotaped models were more effective than those with no models, and some interventions that relied on stronger peer models were also more effective than approaches without modeling. Also important were strategies for corrective feedback. During repeated reading interventions, students benefited from correction of their word-level errors.

In 2003, Kuhn and Stahl reviewed research on fluency development, analyzing 58 studies. They included some studies that were not experimental and therefore took a broader view than the NRP. They found conflicting evidence as to the overall effectiveness of simple unassisted repeated readings—such readings did not always work. Kuhn and Stahl argued that fluency growth comes from increasing the volume of reading that children do, and that this may be accomplished in many ways. They confirmed that the use of a model, which they called a scaffold (a teacher, a computer, a peer), is helpful and also indicated that there seems to be a fluency "time"—the time between initial decoding instruction and a focus on reading to learn. For most children, this is the end of first grade through the end of second grade.

In 2004, Therrien conducted a meta-analysis of the effects of repeated reading on the development of fluency and comprehension. Effect sizes (estimates of educational importance) across studies yielded the following guidelines: Repeated reading to an adult was more effective than repeated reading to a peer, both in building fluency and in building comprehension; to improve fluency on a particular passage, students should be told directly to read to build fluency, to build comprehension, or both before reading the passage three or four times; and, if the goal is to increase general fluency or general comprehension, students should be provided with corrective feedback and should reread until they reach a performance criterion (e.g., 100 words per minute).

FOUNDATIONAL TEACHER KNOWLEDGE

In the area of fluency, then, there are some specific guidelines that come from looking across studies. All fluency work is aimed at increasing comprehension, but fluency-building strategies are not the same as comprehension-building strategies. We are not suggesting that teachers should not care whether students understand texts; generally speaking, though, it is useful to build fluency with texts that children have already understood, or to spend a few moments ensuring comprehension on the initial reading.

Oral reading fluency depends partially upon automaticity with word-level skills. Children with inadequate stores of sight words or weak decoding skills are unlikely to benefit from the fluency practices summarized here. Given word-level success, fluency building should involve texts that are fairly challenging rather than those that children can read easily on their own. If a teacher is providing support (in the form of teacher or peer modeling) it may be appropriate to use grade-level texts, even for children who are struggling. If there is no support (that is, the children are simply reading and rereading), teachers are wise to use simpler texts.

Selections appropriate for fluency practice can be found in many places. One place is within a core program. One simple way to find texts for fluency practice is to revisit texts previously read during instruction. These texts are appropriate for fluency practice; children have experience with the words in those texts and they already understand them. Another simple way to locate texts is to preview; upcoming texts in the core program are appropriate for fluency practice during needs-based instruction, especially for older children whose whole-group instruction will provide more attention to comprehension strategies later.

There are many other sources of texts for fluency practice, and we know of no research studies that provide definitive direction here. The simple (but not easy) advice that we give to teachers is this:

1. Be sure that your readers are achieving well enough at the word level that they can benefit from fluency practice; remember that children who are reading at levels below mid-first grade are better served by explicit work to build their word-level skills when they are in their needs-based groups.

2. Experiment with different levels of teacher scaffolding. Figure 5.1 provides four simple ways to engage children in reading; while scaffolding from a teacher is an important characteristic of effective fluency work, it is possible to have too much of a good thing. Try to match your fluency support with your children's developing skills. If they need the highest level of support (echo reading) provide that, but if they can work in a particular text with only choral or partner reading, do not spend instructional time on unnecessary support.

3. Experiment with texts at various levels of difficulty. It takes relatively little time and effort to ascertain whether the instructional strategies that we are suggesting in this chapter provide enough scaffolding to build fluency for a group of children in a relatively difficult text.

Most support ↓ Least support	Echo reading	The teacher reads a sentence and then the group rereads it aloud.
	Choral reading	The teacher leads the entire group reading aloud in unison.
	Partner reading	Pairs of readers alternate reading aloud by following a specific turn-taking procedure.
	Whisper reading	Each child reads aloud (but not in unison) in a quiet voice.

FIGURE 5.1. Instructional practices that build fluency.

4. Attend to your children's fluency development carefully, and if they are not able to work in grade-level text, even with large amounts of scaffolding, try to move quickly toward that goal.

Fluency activities have one thing in common—they provide repeated reading practice, either with a single text or with multiple texts. They are all designed for transfer to new text. Fluency-building activities provide chances for teachers to document and share progress with students and parents; these data can be collected almost daily during the instruction. Simple charts like the one depicted in Figure 5.2 help to show children that their practice is paying off. Figure 5.3 provides goals for words correct per minute for children performing at the 50th percentile across the grade levels reported by Hasbrouck and Tindal (2006). These goals are useful because there are different goals for different times of year; remember too that we are expecting children to increase their words correct per minute *and* to read increasingly more difficult text. Stopwatches or kitchen timers help engage children in monitoring their own progress and are particularly useful as part of the instructional strategies that we describe next.

TIMED REPEATED READING

As we consider instructional strategies for building fluency, you will see that they are all variations on a theme, and that theme is repeated reading. We will start by describing that strategy, and then we will move to the derivative strategies, each of which incorporates repeated reading somewhat differently.

Name _____

Total seconds							
180							
170							
160							
150							
140							
130							
120							
110							
100							
90							
80							
70							
60							
50							
40							
30							
20							
10							
Times read							
Date							

FIGURE 5.2. Fluency record.

What Kind of Reader Will Timed Repeated Reading Help?

Repeated reading is used with children who have weak reading rates, but adequate decoding strategies and adequate recognition of high-frequency words. For example, if, as first graders, these children were screened with a grade-level oral reading passage, they might score adequately in terms of reading accuracy. However, their reading rate would not be close to that of their higher-achieving peers or to the grade-level goals we listed in Figure 5.3. As second or third graders, they might be as much as 1 year behind, both in terms of reading accuracy and reading rate. In terms of the quality of their reading, it is likely to sound labored and word-by-word, with little attention to punctuation or meaningful phrasing.

What Is the Instructional Focus of Timed Repeated Reading?

Repeated readings provide simple, repetitive oral reading practice on a short passage until the child reaches the criterion of 100 words per minute. The teacher's role is to select the passage, keep time, note word recognition errors, and measure progress toward the criterion. Each time the child reads, rate should increase and errors should decrease.

Where Does Timed Repeated Reading Come from?

This strategy is widely used and widely and generally attributed to S. J. Samuels (1979). Children's success with this strategy formed the basis for many theoretical and practical discussions of cognitive automaticity theory, the notion that the cognitive system used for reading text is a limited-resource system. That is, if many cognitive resources are used for recognizing words, then few would be available to

Grade	Fall	Winter	Spring
1		23	53
2	51	72	89
3	71	92	107
4	94	112	123
5	110	127	139
6	127	140	150
7	128	136	150
8	133	146	151

FIGURE 5.3. Goals for words correct per minute at the 50th percentile. From Hasbrouck and Tindal (2006). Copyright (2006) by the International Reading Association. Reprinted by permission.

do the more complex work of constructing meaning. Thus, repeated reading of text would create more automatic word recognition and facilitate comprehension. In fact, parts of that theory were eventually challenged, particularly the idea that simple repeated reading would be an effective way to build word recognition strategies. A more precise conception of the effects of repeated reading on word recognition is that it may build automaticity with specific words or word patterns that a reader already has the basic word recognition strategies to decode. The speed at which a reader successfully decodes a new word is related to the number of times that he or she has successfully decoded it before. Repeated reading does build reading rate and reading prosody in the passage that is read and reread. However, repeated reading does not substitute for word recognition instruction when that is what an individual reader needs.

What Materials Are Needed for Timed Repeated Reading?

The original recommendations target short (100-word) passages that are slightly above the instructional level of the reader. Since these readers are struggling, consider previously read texts, including excerpts, from the core program. In addition, teachers need a stopwatch or timer and a chart to document progress.

How Do Teachers Prepare for Timed Repeated Reading?

There are three steps in preparing to implement timed repeated readings: Find passages, decide how to calculate and chart progress, and create a rotation so that the teacher can time at least one student each day as others practice their passage. As with most of the instructional strategies in the book, however, we know teachers whose attention to organization in the short run saves time and effort in the long run. Many teachers create a filing system for multiple passages from old stories. Black-line master copies of texts are often provided by core reading programs specifically for this type of reading practice.

Passages can easily be formatted for use in repeated readings by counting off and marking 100-word sections. The reason for that is simple management—if you ask children to work with 100-word sections, and your goal is for them to read 100 words correctly per minute, no calculations are necessary. It is also very easy for children to see their progress toward the goal; given a stopwatch set to indicate 1 minute's time, the children can mark their spot at the bell. Nearly all children will get further on a second reading, and still further on a third.

Of course, the ease of using 100 words does not preclude your use of a longer passage, which might have more integrity in terms of meaning. A simple formula and a calculator can convert reading rates into words per minute in a text of any length.

$$\text{Words per minute} = \frac{\text{Words per minute} \times 60}{\text{Number of seconds}}$$

For example, if you choose a text that is 90 words long, and the child takes 1 minute and 45 seconds to read it, you must convert the time to seconds (105) and then cross-multiply: $90 \times 60 = 5,400$; $5,400/105 = 51.4$ words per minute. We had to use a calculator to get that answer, but it is still a simple procedure. Words correct per minute (a slightly different score) demands one extra calculation—one that can usually be done without a calculator. Take the number of words in the passage, subtract the number of errors that the student made, and enter the result into the equation as the total number of words. Calculating words correct per minute alleviates the potential problem of a child who simply miscalls or invents many words quickly in order to beat the clock.

Finally, you must create a daily rotation so that you can work with one child while others are practicing their passages. This is the time when a chart is most useful for recording student progress.

How Do You Implement Timed Repeated Reading?

When children who need fluency work are gathered in a small group with a teacher, the implementation goal is to have all children reading for the entire time that the group is gathered. Below we present the daily goals from the perspective of a teacher.

- Day 1: Listen to each child in the group and record his or her initial fluency rate.
- Day 2: Have all children practice reading their passages. Time and provide feedback to one child at a time while the other children continue to practice.
- Day 3: Chart progress toward the 100-words-per-minute criterion. As an individual child reaches it, the teacher can provide that child a new passage and begin the sequence again.

A strong organization plan at the outset of a repeated readings implementation allows you to set this strategy in motion, keep all of the children reading (even when they need to be reading different passages), and assess progress during instruction.

How Do You Know If Timed Repeated Reading Is Working?

The 100-words-per-minute criterion is an important benchmark for the success of repeated readings. It is not the only one, however. The goal of this strategy is not to manage movement toward the criterion on each individual passage; it is to increase a child's reading rate by building automaticity of recognition of words that the child can decode. Therefore, repeated readings are successful as a pattern is attained; over time, children should read the passage "cold" (the first time), with a faster rate. Also, the number of times that a child needs to read the passage in order to reach the criterion should decrease. When children begin to transfer their increased rate to new passages, consider providing a more difficult text. When children have adequate rate in grade-level text, discontinue fluency intervention, but continue to monitor progress.

CHORAL PARTNER READING

Repeated readings, as described above, are likely to be useful for many children in need of differentiated work in fluency. What is missing from that procedure, though, is modeling. Choral partner reading includes repetition, but also teacher modeling.

What Kind of Reader Will Choral Partner Reading Help?

As with repeated readings, choral partner readings are designed for children who have at least mid-first-grade word recognition skills. Choral partner reading is not a substitute for letter-sound instruction, letter-pattern instruction, or high-frequency word instruction.

What Is the Instructional Focus of Choral Partner Reading?

Choral partner reading provides students with support from their teacher and peers to develop fluency with short challenging passages. Teachers first model, then students read chorally with partners, then teachers assess progress. This strategy is called choral partner reading because at least two readers are reading at the same time. It differs slightly from paired reading, where pairs of children alternate reading aloud with listening and tracking.

Where Does Choral Partner Reading Come from?

This technique is a more recent adaptation of the neurological impress method (Hollingsworth, 1978), where teachers worked one on one in choral reading with struggling readers, particularly with children in special education. That approach included an unusual form of modeling, in which the teacher whispered into the ear on the child's dominant side—the name "impress" refers to the theory that this form of scaffolding "impressed" the words into the brain of the child. Surely that theory is inconsistent with more current information about how children learn words. The success of the technique can be attributed to the powerful effects of modeling and repetition. The technique is easily adapted and can maximize teacher modeling and reading practice.

What Materials Are Needed for Choral Partner Reading?

Materials for choral partner reading (and any instructional strategy for building fluency) must be gathered and organized in advance. Core reading selections, including black-line masters, are useful. In addition, consider poems for children (which are often short and always provide an opportunity to develop prosody) or commercially prepared fluency materials. For this strategy to work, all children in the same group must be reading the same text, so multiple copies are needed.

How Do You Prepare for Choral Partner Reading?

In addition to the preparation steps for timed repeated readings, one additional preparation step is required. You must carefully teach the procedure below. The key to using small-group time wisely is smooth and repetitive instructional procedures. This time, those procedures apply both to you and to the children as they work in pairs.

How Do You Implement Choral Partner Reading?

In the first reading of the text, you model while the children (all of the children in the small group) track with their finger and try to read along. Then the children begin to reread. In these subsequent readings, the children first read chorally and then begin to read independently. One child is working with you as partner, while the rest of the children are paired up together. Each pair works in the same way. The pair read chorally. Then one partner taps the other to indicate that he is ready to read alone. That child reads until he signals, with another tap, that he is ready for partner reading again. When the teacher serves as partner, clearly it will be the child who taps for solo reading; when two children are reading together, they have to alternate the role of solo reader and the role of choral support reader.

How Do You Know If Choral Partner Reading Is Working?

As in repeated readings, a stopwatch and progress monitoring system must be used in order to document student response to this strategy and to decide when to discontinue it. You should discontinue using choral partner reading in two cases—when there is no progress over time or when progress monitoring indicates that students are achieving grade-level fluency scores.

FLUENCY DEVELOPMENT LESSON

Sometimes assessment scores in a classroom will indicate that nearly all children have basic decoding skills and strategies, but that very few have achieved adequate reading fluency. We expect that this is a typical developmental phase, especially at the beginning of second grade. The fluency development lesson can be an appropriate choice if this is the case.

What Kind of Reader Will the Fluency Development Lesson Help?

The fluency development lesson differs from timed repeated readings and from choral partner readings at one basic level—it is more appropriate for larger groups of children. Scaffolding (in the form of modeling) and practice (in the form of repeated reading) are still included, but there is no initial assessment phase, so teachers can use this strategy with a larger group (seven or eight children) or even with the whole class.

What Is the Instructional Focus of the Fluency Development Lesson?

This technique is very similar to the fluency practices that are typically part of the core instructional program in kindergarten and first grade, when teachers read to children from big books. The focus is on developing accuracy, rate, and prosody for a specific, short passage.

Where Does the Fluency Development Lesson Come from?

This technique was developed by Tim Rasinski and his colleagues (Rasinksi, Padak, Linek, & Sturtevant, 1994) for use with elementary-age children. The 1994 study was conducted in second grade, clearly within the fluency window that Kuhn and Stahl (2003) recommended. Readers in second grade have likely developed basic word recognition strategies and a reasonable store of sight words; they are ready to apply these skills with greater speed and accuracy.

What Materials Are Needed for the Fluency Development Lesson?

Short passages that are slightly above the instructional level are needed for fluency development lessons. In the original study, the authors reported using poems. In fact, there are many commercial sources containing sets of poems that might be used; core program materials, particularly for second graders, also provide multiple copies of texts that can be used to implement this strategy.

How Do You Prepare for the Fluency Development Lesson?

Simply gathering materials and thinking about management are the keys to fluency development lessons. Teachers who organize materials for any one of the fluency strategies in this chapter can use those same materials with a different instructional strategy.

How Do You Implement the Fluency Development Lesson?

As in choral partner reading, fluency development lessons occur in a 3-day cycle.

- Day 1: Model expressive reading of the entire passage, with adequate rate and prosody; children track in their personal copies. Children choral read, then echo read with the teacher.
- Day 2: Children read orally in pairs, alternating pages. If the entire passage is long, children practice reading a specific 100-word passage that the teacher has selected.
- Day 3: Children continue to practice in their pairs while the teacher assesses fluency for each child on the 100-word selection.

With a larger group or a more difficult passage, the cycle could be expanded to 4 days, with 2 days for student practice and teacher assessment.

How Do You Know If the Fluency Development Lesson Is Working?

Continuous assessment of fluency is important, but not more important than increasing reading practice. In fact, any teacher's first priority must be to keep the children reading and rereading in an engaged way. We recommend that you use the first few rounds of fluency development lessons to establish the procedures that the children will use to work together. Once that management piece is set, you can focus attention on assessment of progress. Because you might be using this approach with a slightly larger group, the use of 100-word passages makes assessment much simpler; the actual procedure of assessing the number of words correct in 1 minute takes exactly 1 minute of oral reading per child. A chart to monitor progress over time makes those precious minutes worthwhile for instructional decision making.

FLUENCY-ORIENTED READING INSTRUCTION

You will see traces of repeated readings, choral partner readings, and fluency development lessons in this instructional strategy. Fluency-oriented reading instruction (FORI), though, is the most comprehensive of the strategies we present in this chapter. You can used it in a needs-based group, to be sure, but also with a whole class.

What Kind of Reader Will FORI Help?

This strategy is appropriate for second-grade children who begin the year at least at mid-first-grade level. Building phonics and other word recognition skills for students with weaker lower-level skills where they are weak is a prerequisite to using this instructional strategy.

What Is the Instructional Focus of FORI?

FORI provides students with varied support across an instructional week. It is designed for whole classes but can also easily be implemented in needs-based groups targeting fluency practice. The important difference between this strategy and others that we have described is that this one was designed to provide scaffolding in the form of various types of modeling and practice with core-program selections. You will see, too, that there is a built-in emphasis on comprehension at the beginning of the cycle; the strategy assumes that the stories will be unfamiliar and interesting and that children will profit from initial discussion.

Where Does FORI Come from?

This procedure has been tested recently with second graders (Stahl & Heubach, 2005). It is also being used in a large-scale study; we await results.

What Materials Are Needed for FORI?

This program was designed and tested as an instructional strategy to be applied to a core reading program in a district where all children were required to use the same materials. The study required that children have their basal anthologies at school and also that they take them home (and the researchers specifically note that students did not lose their books!). In lieu of sending the hardback books home, you could use black-line master versions, which are often included with core series.

How Do You Prepare for FORI?

As there is no need for finding new texts, teachers can spend their preparation time carefully thinking through the procedures. The key to FORI is assigning children to partners and teaching the partners to engage productively in oral partner reading. The only other preparation required is the selection of an extension activity for children to use each Friday.

How Do You Implement FORI?

FORI was designed on a 5-day cycle since that rotation is the most common way that core materials are organized.

- Day 1: Read the selection aloud to the class and lead a comprehension-focused discussion.
- Day 2: Engage children in echo reading. Children take the selection home to read with a caregiver.
- Day 3: Read the selection chorally. Children again practice at home with a caregiver.
- Day 4: Students partner-read story. Children have a final chance to practice at home.
- Day 5: Children do extension activities. As they work, assess the fluency of each child individually by having him or her read the story aloud.

How Do You Know If FORI Is Working?

The Friday procedure is specifically designed to build continuous assessment into the instructional routine. These assessments can help you monitor oral reading fluency over time. Progress monitoring with transfer passages can also be accomplished during partner reading. Remember that the goal of fluency-building practices is for all students to reach at least grade-level criterion measures with grade-level texts. Use of the goals in Figure 5.3 can help teachers to monitor progress toward that goal. Remember, in general, that your target must be high levels of rate and accuracy and also appropriate prosody; while you measure reading rate, do not ignore the other components of reading fluency.

TO LEARN MORE

Our experience suggests that teachers who begin to use assessments and to engage in differentiated instruction will be particularly aware of their children's progress toward fluency goals. Remember, though, that initial word recognition instruction and fluency building are two different instructional goals and that they are not appropriate for the same children. Children will need to pursue these goals in sequence.

We imagine that many of you will want to read more about fluency. Rasinksi's (2003) *The Fluent Reader: Oral Reading Strategies for Building Word*

Recognition, Fluency, and Comprehension is a very popular book that we have used with teacher study groups. Also consider a subscription to *The Reading Teacher*. Information about subscription is available on the International Reading Association's website *(www.reading.org)*. Nonsubscribers can also buy individual articles for a small fee, and they are sent immediately via e-mail attachment. You might also encourage your school to subscribe as part of the professional library. Recently, there have been many wonderful articles that might build your understanding of reading fluency. Hudson, Lane, and Pullen (2005) describe relationships between fluency and comprehension, recommend several assessments for measuring reading fluency, and describe eight commercial resources. Pikulski and Chard (2005) provide a cogent discussion of why and how alphabet knowledge and decoding strategies ultimately contribute to reading fluency. They also make a case for considering the correlational research that documents the relationship between reading volume and vocabulary, and we consider that a very important concept. Melanie Kuhn (2004) describes a second-grade small-group project that included both the practices we have described and also wide reading. We invite you to continue to learn about reading fluency, and *The Reading Teacher* is an excellent way to stay current.

CHAPTER 6

Building Vocabulary

In Chapter 4 we described instructional strategies for building word recognition, but word recognition strategies for young children are only appropriate for words in their meaning vocabulary—words that, if pronounced orally, the child can match with meaning. Phonics instruction without vocabulary knowledge, then, is meaningless. In this chapter we turn our attention to strategies for building oral vocabulary, for increasing and connecting the words that a child stores in his or her mental lexicon. The general goal of increasing conceptual and word knowledge is one that no one disputes. Perhaps one of the most important reasons why teachers need to pay attention to vocabulary is that vocabulary knowledge has a spiraling effect. The more words you know, the easier it is to learn yet more words (Stahl & Nagy, 2005). How teachers accomplish that goal, though, is another matter. In this chapter, we will present some fairly simple ways to build differentiation of vocabulary instruction into your needs-based routines.

One of the most persistent questions about vocabulary instruction is whether it is better to teach a limited number of words fully and directly or to expose children to a large number of words to increase the potential for incidental learning. Marzano (2004) sums up the argument nicely. Those who argue for wide reading do so because vocabulary size and the amount a child reads are correlated—children who read more do know more words, so they must learn them from reading—and given the total number of words that children need to learn each year, it is impossible to account for them through direct vocabulary instruction. Those who argue for direct instruction do so on the basis of two other claims: context is generally unreliable as a means of inferring word meanings and most words occur too infrequently to provide the number of exposures needed to learn them.

Marzano, though, takes a middle ground that we find entirely sensible. Do both. Provide children with opportunities for incidental learning during wide reading and rich exposure to language and also provide direct instruction in word meanings.

The NRP's (National Institute of Child Health and Human Development, 2000) synthesis of research (*www.nationalreadingpanel.org/Publications/publications.htm*) included a chapter on the development of vocabulary in classrooms. That report concluded that teaching vocabulary directly improves both vocabulary and comprehension ability in general, and that teaching word meanings before reading improves comprehension of a specific text. Many instructional strategies are potentially effective for accomplishing these goals; they tend to include definitions, contextual information, and repetition. Unfortunately, most of the studies reviewed in the NRP report were conducted with older students. As careful consumers of research, we must be cautious about applying results from studies conducted with one population of individuals to another.

RECENT RESEARCH AND REVIEWS

Another research team (Jitendra, Edwards, Sacks, & Jacobson, 2004) reviewed research on vocabulary instruction for students with learning disabilities—a population excluded from the NRP review. As in the NRP review, the studies they located (19 in all) were mostly conducted with students in grades 4 and above. Studies that taught students to use keywords or mnemonic strategies to create both visual and auditory links were effective with students with LDs. Studies that used semantic maps and feature analyses to categorize words by similarities and differences in meaning were also effective. Clearly, all studies show that deeper instruction leads to larger vocabulary gains, certainly in the case of struggling readers.

Another interesting study considered the type and amount of oral language to which preschool-age children have access in their homes. Hart and Risley's (1995) careful and compelling study of this issue used tape-recorded interactions during family time in homes that represented three levels of socioeconomic advantage. The least-advantaged children were engaged in less rich language interactions, mostly centered on everyday business. The most advantaged also experienced a language advantage—parents engaged in more extended language interactions, stretching and extending child language. That early vocabulary infusion can lead to persistent language advantage.

We are continually asked whether there are lists of words that should be learned at different grade levels. Biemiller and Slonim (2001) investigated the question of the rate of vocabulary acquisition and also whether specific words are learned in a predictable order. These researchers used a word list compiled by Edgar Dale in 1981, the *Living Word Vocabulary,* and tested three different samples of children to determine which words they knew and to describe word learning from grades 2 through 12. They estimated vocabulary knowledge at third grade and again at fifth grade and then computed the average number of words learned. They found that between grades 3 and 5 children added about three new root word meanings to their vocabularies each day and that word learning progressed at a fairly predictable rate. However, at the outset, there were large differences in word knowledge among third graders, suggesting that not all children had similar rates of learning prior to grade 3. They also found that the growth in root word knowledge is relatively developmental—children tend to learn word roots in roughly the same order, even though the children have different types and amounts of access to words through reading and listening.

The work of Biemiller and Slonim highlights a major concern—the fact that students do not begin school on an equal vocabulary footing. It is likely that vocabulary interventions can help bridge the gap? Recent evidence is encouraging. Collins (2005) explored vocabulary acquisition from read-alouds for 4-year-old English language learners (ELLs). Children in the experimental condition heard teachers read aloud from storybooks three times over the course of 3 weeks. During reading, the teacher stopped to explain a set of target words. Explanations included providing a definition, suggesting a synonym, making a gesture, and offering a sentence context different from the one in the story. Control students heard the same books, but teachers did not explain the target words. Students receiving the explanations learned more of the target words. Although students with higher levels of English language knowledge learned more of the words, even those with the lowest levels outperformed the control students. This study indicates that storybook reading can be effective in building vocabulary even for preschoolers with very little knowledge of English. (Incidentally, this study was awarded the International Reading Association's Outstanding Dissertation Award for 2005.)

Justice, Meier, and Walpole (2005) also investigated word learning from storybook reading, this time with at-risk kindergarteners. All of the children selected for the study had both low alphabet knowledge and low listening vocabulary knowledge. Children were randomly assigned to treatment and control conditions. In the experimental condition, children listened to a total of 10 storybooks read four times each over a period of 10 weeks. Six target words were selected from each text. During reading, three of the words were explained, and three were not. Results indicated that children participating in the read-alouds did not learn new vocabulary words simply from exposure, but they did learn more new words if they were explained during reading. In addition, the lowest-vocabulary children in the treatment made the largest gains. As this study once again shows, explaining of word meanings during read-alouds is a viable, research-based way to build vocabulary knowledge and it is preferable to simple read-alouds, even when repeated.

If explaining word meanings during read-alouds is good, still better is encouraging children to interact as the meanings are explained. Brabham and Lynch-Brown (2002) conducted a study of the effects of reading aloud on vocabulary and comprehension for first- and third-grade students. They used informational storybooks, a hybrid genre with content information presented in a narrative structure. For one group, "just reading," these researchers used a brief prereading introduction, read the texts aloud without interruption, and then asked the children to write or draw after reading. For another group, "performance reading," they used the same prereading instruction, but invited children to ask questions about the story before and after an uninterrupted read-aloud. After reading, teachers engaged children in a postreading discussion. For the third group, "interactive reading," researchers used the same prereading discussion, but invited children to make comments and ask questions during reading. Postreading discussion followed the same format as the performance group. Results indicated that both first- and third-grade students learned some vocabulary in the just-reading condition, more in the performance-reading condition, and most in the interactive-reading condition. Effects on comprehension were very small. Findings indicate support for interaction and explanation during read-alouds to facilitate word learning.

Much remains to be learned about vocabulary instruction in the early grades, but the research reported above suggests that read-alouds are a very important context for word learning and that teachers must maximize talk about new words (both in terms of their own explanations and in terms of student discussion) in order to maximize the effects of storybook reading on vocabulary development.

FOUNDATIONAL TEACHER KNOWLEDGE

What does it mean to know a word, anyway? Actually, that question is quite complex. Word knowledge is not an all-or-nothing proposition. In fact, a particular word might be at any one of several "phases" of familiarity for an individual. At the low end is no knowledge—there are many words that an individual simply has never encountered meaningfully and for which he or she has absolutely no frame of reference. Another corpus of words in an individual's lexicon is associated with vague meanings—there is some emerging sense of the word. Other words exist in a context-dependent state; an individual knows them only when they are presented in a rich, supportive, and specific context. Still other words are known, but it is difficult for the individual to recall the word meaning quickly enough for it to be useful. And finally, the "known" words are those that an individual knows deeply and can explain fairly automatically with definition and connections to other words and concepts. Figure 6.1 orders these phases and is based on the work of Beck, McKeown, and Kucan (2002).

Phase	Characteristics
1	No knowledge of the word's meaning
2	Vague sense of the word's meaning
3	Narrow knowledge of the word's meaning, with the aid of context
4	Good knowledge of the word's meaning but shaky, unreliable recall
5	Thorough, decontextualized knowledge of the word and its connections with other words

FIGURE 6.1. Phases of knowing a word. Based on Beck, McKeown, and Kucan (2002).

Before we discuss how to teach word meanings, it makes sense to answer a more basic question: Given limited time for direct instruction in word meanings, exactly which words should we teach? There are two general arguments (and, again, they are probably best combined). One is that we should teach words that are easiest for children to learn. Think of words as labels for concepts. Graves (1986) argued that there are three types of words to be learned. In the first case, the child already knows the spoken form of the word and concept it represents, but cannot recognize the written form. In this instance, it is relatively easy to teach the written form. For example, it is easy to teach the word *bird* because a beginning reader already knows the concept and can recognize the spoken form of the word. This is one goal of word recognition instruction. The second category of words is really our target in the elementary school vocabulary-building curriculum. In this case, the child knows the concept in general and knows related concepts, but does not know the spoken word. For example, it is simple for a child who knows the word *happy* to learn the word *delighted*. This is because the idea of being very happy already exists in the mind of the child even though no word is yet attached to this idea. And the last category of words, the most difficult to teach, includes words for which the child has very little prior knowledge—the child knows neither the spoken word nor the concept it represents. In the elementary school curriculum, such words often include content area terms, like *metamorphosis* and *democracy*. These concepts and their labels must be developed together in rich instructional designs. Figure 6.2 depicts the three types of words in the form of a diagram. If you examine it carefully, you will realize that every word in the English language falls into one of the three regions. Which words fall where, however, will vary from one person to the next. (We have chosen our examples based on our experience with "typical" beginning readers, but these examples would not be true for all beginning readers.)

If we followed the approach of teaching the easiest words first, we might work from the inside out. Instruction would begin with the innermost region of Figure 6.2, then move to the middle region, and finally to the outermost. Or, we

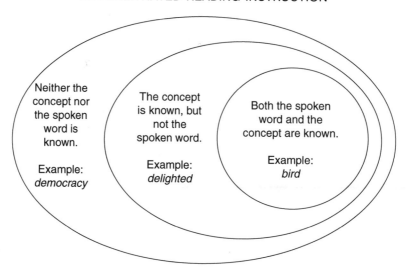

FIGURE 6.2. Three types of vocabulary words.

might teach words from all three areas but select far more from the innermost than from the other regions.

The second argument concerning which words to teach is not based on the ease of learning the words, but rather on their relative utility. Beck et al. (2002) have suggested three tiers, or levels, of words based on their usefulness. Tier 1 words are the most familiar, encompassing roughly 8,000 *word families*. These are words likely to be known by an average third grader. They are used frequently in oral language and are likely to be learned incidentally during school or in informal exchanges outside of school. Examples of Tier 1 words are *park*, *birthday*, and *washing machine*. Tier 2 words are more colorful. They comprise about 7,000 word families. What is special about them is that they are particularly important to academic success. They include words like *fortunate*, *ridiculous*, and *greedy*; they might be included in readings across texts and across contexts. Finally, the largest body of words, the Tier 3 words, includes the rarest words, the 73,500 word families used primarily in one content area context. Examples of Tier 3 words are *isotope* and *estuary*.

In the sections that follow, we present research-based strategies for teaching word meanings. Our approach, at first, is to focus on building oral vocabulary rather than reading vocabulary. You will see that the strategies that we have chosen highlight opportunities for building meaning vocabulary that are presented in storybook reading. Many of these strategies can be used in either whole-group or small-group instruction. Remember, however, that if you teach vocabulary during small-group instruction, children will have more chances to interact with you and with the words, increasing the effectiveness of your instruction.

TEACHING TIER 2 WORDS

What Kind of Reader Will Teaching Tier 2 Words Help?

Young children and children with weak vocabularies benefit from direct instruction in word meanings that occur with reasonably high frequency and are not typically encountered in oral language. Remember that Tier 2 words are those words that are not part of oral language and not part of content-area instruction, but rather serve to enhance and specify word meanings across a variety of contexts. Children who have had relatively little exposure to storybook readings in the preschool years are likely to benefit from this technique, as they will not have had extensive exposure to Tier 2 words.

What Is the Instructional Focus of Teaching Tier 2 Words?

The instructional focus is development of oral vocabulary knowledge, in the context of read-alouds, for words that are neither especially easy (Tier 1) nor especially rare and related to content-area study (Tier 3). The approach relies on storybooks as sources to identify and teach such words. The words are first encountered during storybook read-alouds, and then taught directly after the story.

Where Does Teaching Tier 2 Words Come from?

The concept of Tier 2 words and the instructional technique that we are recommending both come from *Bringing Words to Life: Robust Vocabulary Instruction* (Beck et al., 2002). The authors of that text combine the results of many vocabulary studies and also describe their own work with storybook read-alouds for young children.

What Materials Are Needed for Teaching Tier 2 Words?

Materials needed for teaching Tier 2 words are available in all school libraries. Teachers simply need a set of narrative and information books that are appropriate for read-alouds for children at their grade level. Such books are ones that the students would not be able to read on their own and that contain some words that at least half of the students in class neither recognize nor understand. Books without this level of challenging vocabulary are inappropriate for this strategy.

How Do You Prepare for Teaching Tier 2 Words?

The most important step in preparing to teach Tier 2 words is to select them. There is no "right" or "wrong" answer as to which words to select, except the general conceptual recommendation about what Tier 2 words actually are. Remember that these are words that are unlikely to be learned in oral language exchanges but likely to be seen again in other reading contexts. Consider selecting three Tier 2 words for instruction after reading; other words that are Tier 3 or especially important to understanding the text can be explained through brief discussion during reading.

Once you have selected the words, use a dictionary to construct child-friendly definitions and to consider ways to explain the words in a variety of contexts. You may want to record your words and definitions on chart paper or sentence strips so that you can use them easily during instruction. Teachers we know put library pockets into the backs of the books to share their read-aloud books and Tier 2 selections across classrooms.

How Do You Implement Teaching Tier 2 Words?

Remember that Tier 2 words are taught after reading. Engage children in an interactive read-aloud focusing attention on comprehension and enjoyment of the story. During reading, briefly explain any words that would be a barrier to comprehension of the text. After reading, lead a discussion of the text.

After you have finished the read-aloud, you can teach the Tier 2 words you have chosen. The procedure is simple, repetitive, and interactive.

1. Say the word and ask the children to repeat it. "We are going to learn the word _____ . Say the word."
2. Describe the word as it was used in the book. "In our story, the author used the word _____ to _____ ."
3. Tell the definition directly. "The word _____ means _____ ."
4. Provide two uses of the word in different contexts than that of the story.
5. Engage the children in several additional examples.
6. Have the students repeat the word.

In the days and weeks following the read-aloud, look for opportunities to revisit the words you have taught. Your record-keeping system (a list of the words somewhere in the room) will help you recall which words you've taught, how long ago, and how many times you've returned to them.

How Do You Know If Teaching Tier 2 Words Is Working?

Remember that your goal with Tier 2 words is to build your children's oral vocabularies. You know that this strategy is working when students can understand previously taught words in new contexts or when they use the words in their own oral language. You can monitor their knowledge by systematically returning to words previously taught.

ELL STORYBOOK INTERVENTION

What Kind of Reader Will ELL Storybook Intervention Help?

One group of children who have pronounced needs in oral language development are ELLs. This strategy was proposed as a 30-minute daily intervention for ELLs. It is likely that such a strategy would also be appropriate for English-speaking kindergarten and first-grade children with weak oral vocabulary and language skills. In fact, we can see no difference in the strategies that are designed for first- and second-language children; high-quality vocabulary instruction is likely to benefit all.

What Is the Instructional Focus of ELL Storybook Intervention?

This strategy is designed to enhance listening vocabulary and content knowledge, listening comprehension, and oral expression. You will see that it shares many similarities with the Tier 2 word instruction described above. The difference is that this strategy does not assume that the children already understand the storybook that is read aloud; more attention is paid to comprehension of the entire book.

Where Does ELL Storybook Intervention Come from?

This strategy was described in a journal article that did not include any data on its effectiveness (Hickman, Pollard-Durodola, & Vaughn, 2004); experimental evidence on vocabulary instruction for ELLs is scant. Instead, the article includes references to other works on vocabulary and comprehension instruction as well as to instruction for ELLs. The strategy, though, is well described and conceptually sound, so we think it is a good one to consider for small-group differentiated instruction.

What Materials Are Needed for ELL Storybook Intervention?

Like teaching Tier 2 words, this strategy teaches vocabulary through read-alouds. Teachers need to select narrative and information books of approximately 1,000 words. The authors suggest that the books be grouped by theme, so that the children can connect ideas and revisit words across texts. Since the books are to be read aloud by the teacher, it is important that they are not books that the children could read on their own; the words in the books should be more complex than those that are already in the children's reading vocabularies.

Teachers need to choose a place in the classroom for display of the words. A bulletin board or chart paper list would be easy to set up and use. The important thing is that both the teacher and the students have cues to review and remember the words that they have studied, facilitating their recognition in new contexts.

How Do You Prepare for ELL Storybook Intervention?

If possible, choose the stories and group them by theme so that there is maximum potential for vocabulary transfer. For example, a group of texts might include several fantasy stories with frogs as main characters and then several information books about the life cycle of frogs; such texts would tend to share a corpus of words.

Next, break each story into segments, choosing passages of approximately 200–250 words that also represent logical breaks in the text. Breaking the story into segments will allow you to focus attention on language interactions during your small-group instruction. Choose three Tier 2 words to teach for each text segment. Prepare definitions and contextual examples for the words.

How Do You Implement ELL Storybook Intervention?

This strategy, as it was designed for ELLs, included vocabulary instruction before, during, and after reading. The strategy as defined below assumes that you have one text, broken into four segments, read over the course of a week. You read each text segment aloud twice the day it is first introduced, and then you read the entire text aloud (including all of the segments) on the final day.

- Days 1–4: Introduce the day's segment. Preteach the words chosen for that segment. Read the text segment aloud to the children. Check for student comprehension by using explicit and inferential questions. Encourage discussion. Review the vocabulary words. Reread the text selection, this time stopping to fully discuss each vocabulary word as it appears in the text.
- Day 5: Review several of the words that have proved most difficult. Reread the entire text. Review all of the words.

How Do You Know If ELL Storybook Intervention Is Working?

As children encounter previously taught words in new texts and contexts, they should notice them and be able to understand them. Because this strategy is used with small groups, you have the chance to engage your ELL children or your children with weak vocabularies in extended oral responses; you will see that their ability to use language improves, but not as quickly as their ability to understand it. Be alert to opportunities to assess students' knowledge of taught words as they appear in future texts; that is the ultimate assessment of the effectiveness of this strategy.

CONCEPT OF DEFINITION

What Kind of Reader Will Concept of Definition Help?

Sometimes you will have to develop knowledge of Tier 3 words—words for which students have much less background. Concept of definition is a strategy useful for developing an understanding of words that represent entirely new concepts for young learners. It is likely to be especially useful for teaching content-specific vocabulary important to grade-level goals.

What Is the Instructional Focus of Concept of Definition?

The focus of this strategy is building conceptual knowledge by teaching new concepts in direct relationship to known ones. This strategy relies on the creation of a semantic organizer and is sometimes called word mapping. The word map that is created in the course of this instruction makes explicit the connections of a new word to known words and concepts.

Where Does Concept of Definition Come from?

This instructional strategy is based on an ancient idea, first discussed by Aristotle. He suggested that the definition of a noun must include the category to which the concept belongs as well as features that distinguish it from other members of that category. The notion of using a simple diagram to teach these relationships is far newer (Schwartz & Raphael, 1985).

What Materials Are Needed for Concept of Definition?

In order to implement this strategy, you need a word map that allows students to show connections. This word map might be drawn on the board, presented with an overhead projector, or duplicated on paper for students to use. A simple word map has a space for the word, the connections to its superordinate category (the class to which it belongs), its characteristics or attributes, and some examples. Figure 6.3 provides an example of such a map. In it, the word *poultry* is shown to be a member of the category meats. Specific characteristics are provided along with three examples.

How Do You Prepare for Concept of Definition?

This strategy is only useful when the target word is a member of a specific category, with particular characteristics and examples. However, many content-area terms are of this kind! The strategy is useful both for developing new concepts and also for teaching children to generate definitions as they are learning new words.

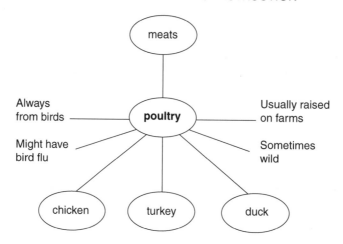

FIGURE 6.3. Example of a word map.

How Do You Implement Concept of Definition?

This strategy is implemented first with known concepts so that children grow accustomed to how the word maps work. Then, gradually, it is used to teach less familiar concepts. For example, you could introduce word maps with the concept of a flower, with which the students are already familiar. The word map would indicate that a flower is a type of plant and that flowers have petals, stems, leaves, and roots. The map might include roses and daisies as examples of flowers. In presenting the map, you would point out that grass (among other types of plants) is not included because it is not a flower.

Once students understand what a word map is, you can use this strategy to teach words and concepts directly as part of your content-area instruction, or you can use it either before or after a read-aloud. We do not think it would be appropriate during a read-aloud, as teaching an individual word might take as long as 5 minutes—too long to stop during reading without compromising comprehension.

How Do You Know If Concept of Definition Is Working?

You know this strategy is working when children show evidence that they have learned the concepts targeted and when they can use the map on their own or during discussion to formulate and remember definitions. As with all vocabulary strategies, the goal is to teach the particular words deeply and also to teach word-learning strategies so that children can benefit more from incidental word-learning opportunities.

SEMANTIC FEATURE ANALYSIS

An instructional approach that is a close cousin to the concept of definition is semantic feature analysis (feature analysis, for short). This technique involves a simple chart that lists members of the same category together with their features. The chart may be connected with a particular text, or it may be part of a lesson in which a cluster of new words is presented without a written context.

What Kind of Reader Will Feature Analysis Help?

Feature analysis has been used successfully with all kinds of readers, from proficient to struggling. We have watched second-grade teachers use it effectively and suspect that teachers of kindergarten and first grade could make it work with picture support and plenty of oral explanation.

What Is the Instructional Focus of Feature Analysis?

This approach, like so many of the best vocabulary techniques, introduces words in a related cluster. It is an excellent way to compare and contrast members of the same category and also to grasp the two elements of a good definition: the category to which a concept belongs and the features that distinguish it from other members of that category. In fact, after students become involved in this activity, they can craft definitions of their own from a completed feature analysis chart.

Where Does Feature Analysis Come from?

Feature analysis was first suggested by Dale Johnson and David Pearson (1984) in their classic book on vocabulary instruction. A more recent book-length treatment of this well-researched approach was written by Susan Pittelman and her colleagues (Pittelman, Heimlich, Berglund, & French, 1991).

What Materials Are Needed for Feature Analysis?

All you need is a list of nouns that represent members of the same category, a set of markers, and some means of displaying the words in a small chart, such as a whiteboard or piece of chart paper. Butcher paper can be used with younger students, who may prefer to build a larger chart on the floor. (Word cards are not necessary since the words will not be moved once they become part of the chart.)

ᴊu Prepare for Feature Analysis?

ant to think through the words you plan to introduce, making sure that l nouns and all members of the same category. For example, a unit of nsects would be an ideal time to give students who may be struggling with ._ concepts a chance to study word relationships through feature analysis. Insects are a good example of a category that includes several members the class may be studying. Figure 6.4 shows how one second-grade teacher organized such a chart. You must decide in advance what features to include as column headings, making sure that these features are presented in the text or through discussion.

How Do You Implement Feature Analysis?

For students who are relatively unfamiliar with semantic feature analysis, you will need to explain how the chart works after you have introduced the concepts. Following the unit on insects, you would say, "Now we are going to make a little chart that puts some of our insect words together." Point to the first column. "Right here, we are going to write the names of some insects. Who can think of one of the insects we learned about?" You may want to draw a picture of each insect as well. Once the first column is complete, point to the top row. "Next we are going to write some of the things insects may have." It may be best to fill in these

Insects	Wings	6 legs	Pest
ant	—	+	s
bee	+	+	—
cockroach	—	+	+
butterfly	+	+	—

FIGURE 6.4. Feature analysis chart used to teach about insects in second grade.

column headings yourself, explaining them as you go. Once you've done so, say, "Now let's think about ants. Do ants have wings?" When the children say no, place a minus sign in the cell. "I'm going to write a minus sign here because ants do not have wings." Indicating the next column, say, "Do ants have six legs?" When the children say yes, place a plus sign in the cell. "I'm going to write a plus sign because ants always have six legs." Moving to the last column, ask the children, "Are ants pests? By *pests*, I mean, do ants cause us any trouble?" Here, the children may have different opinions based on their experiences. "Well, since it seems that ants are sometimes pests, I'm going to write the letter *s*, for *sometimes*." Complete the other rows, with student input, in the same manner. Once the technique becomes more familiar, you will not need to explain the symbols each time, and the process will go more quickly. In fact, students can eventually work together to complete a feature analysis chart.

The strength of feature analysis lies in discussing the chart after it is completed. In this example, you might prompt children to infer that all insects have six legs. ("What does every insect seem to have?") You can also engage the group in contrasting any pair of insects. They can conclude, for instance, that bees and butterflies have exactly the same features. "Does this mean that bees and butterflies are the same?" you might ask. When the children insist they are different, ask in what way. Someone is sure to say that bees sting and butterflies don't. You might add another column, labeled "Stinger," so that you can write a plus sign for bee and a minus for butterfly. You can also lead the children in building definitions from the chart. Teach them to define any category member, first by naming the category and then by listing its features. Point to the portions of the chart as you create examples. "Let's see," you might say, "from our chart we could say that a butterfly is an insect that has wings and six legs and that is not a pest."

How Do You Know If Feature Analysis Is Working?

Look for signs that children are catching on to how a feature analysis chart works. You might prompt responses that will tell you this. ("So, if ants have six legs, what should I write here?") A second sign is whether the children can eventually complete a feature analysis chart on their own. Once they can, you will have given them a powerful tool for exploring relationships among category members—a skill that is especially useful in content subjects.

CONCEPT SORTING

Once a set of words have been introduced, children can sort word cards as they review them in small-group settings. Such review serves two purposes: it reinforces the meanings of individual words and it builds connections among them.

What Kind of Reader Will Concept Sorting Help?

Children with limited meaning vocabulary, including English language learners, may experience difficulties in easily acquiring new words. This is because their existing vocabularies often do not contain enough familiar words to form the basis of learning new ones.

What Is the Instructional Focus of Concept Sorting?

Concept sorting stresses the meanings of a small set of new words. While the technique is flexible enough to target advanced categorization of abstract concepts, we recommend it here as a means of getting the youngest readers to link new words to concepts they know.

Where Does Concept Sorting Come from?

We believe that the first clear attention to word sorting can be traced to Hilda Taba's technique, called list-group-label (1967). Taba had upper elementary students in mind and technical social studies terminology as a target. A more general approach to sorting, and one clearly useful with primary-age students, was described by Gillet and Kita (1979). Their ideas were greatly elaborated by Donald Bear and his colleagues in *Words Their Way* (2004), a book that we believe represents the most thorough overall treatment of word sorting (not only for vocabulary reinforcement but for work with phonics and spelling as well).

What Materials Are Needed for Concept Sorting?

The words you will use in a concept sort can range in number, depending on the age and language proficiency of your needs-based group. Kindergarteners with limited listening vocabularies will profit from working with as few as five to six word cards. Struggling third graders may be able to work with three times that many. The words you choose must have some connection, but they need not be members of the same category (a limiting requirement of feature analysis). The best words are from Tier 2—general vocabulary terms that children are not likely to pick up from incidental contact. The words could be drawn from vocabulary that students encounter in core selections, and examining the scope and sequence may lead to listings of such words. More frequently, we suspect, you will be able to identify these words by closely reading each selection and noting words that will be important for students to know in future contexts and that are not associated with content subjects.

How Do You Prepare for Concept Sorting?

Once you have chosen a set of words, decide on categories into which the words can be grouped. It is important that these categories be familiar to the children. The word cards displayed in Figure 6.5 are Tier 2 words that concern moods and feelings. Three categories account for all of the word cards: sad, glad, and mad illustrated in Figure 6.6. That is not the only way to categorize them, of course, but you must think of several useful categories before the small-group lesson.

How Do You Implement Concept Sorting?

Gillet and Kita (1979) describe two approaches to a concept sort: open and closed. In an open sort, children are presented with the cards and asked to arrange them into groups on the basis of meaning. In a closed sort, the category labels are supplied in advance by the teacher, and the students' task is to move each word card to the appropriate category. Clearly, open sorts are more demanding than closed sorts. We believe that closed sorts are the better choice for primary-age children with limited listening vocabularies.

Begin by telling the children that they will be putting the words they have been studying into groups. Next, review the word meanings by displaying each card in turn, pronouncing the word, and giving a brief definition and sentence context. "This is the word *furious*. It means very, very mad. The man was furious when the dog bit him. Furious. This is the word *angry*. It is another word for *mad*. She was angry when she didn't get to go to the party." When you finish reviewing the words, introduce the categories. "Some of these words tell about how we feel when we are mad, some tell how we feel when we're sad, and some tell how we feel when we're glad. I'll put these three words here." Place them next to one another, away from the word deck. "Now, where would you put this word? This is *angry*."

It is important to pronounce the words whenever you refer to a card. This is because the idea is not to teach them as sight words (though that may eventually be the result) but to teach their meanings as listening vocabulary. Since this activity requires visual manipulatives (the word cards), the students must know what is

furious	glum	angry	enraged
gloomy	joyful	pleased	dejected
tickled	elated	cheerful	blue

FIGURE 6.5. Word cards for a concept sort.

FIGURE 6.6. Category labels with pictures for a concept sort based on Figure 6.5.

on each card if they are to sort successfully. A wordless variation of this approach is to use picture cards alone. The wordless approach works well as long as there is a clear pictorial referent.

How Do You Know If Concept Sorting Is Working?

Students will eventually encounter the sorted words in future contexts. This is your chance to check whether they remember the meanings. Your follow-up can be more systematic as well. As you present each group of words, put it aside for later review. Make it a point to return to previous sorts as time permits. These review sorts should proceed quickly. They will give you a good idea of whether word meanings are being retained and they will distribute children's exposure to the words—a key to remembering them.

TO LEARN MORE

We believe that fostering vocabulary development is Challenge No. 1 facing teachers of struggling students in the primary grades. Teaching children to decode and to read with fluency is indispensable, to be sure, but unless vocabulary growth keeps pace, the prospects of becoming a successful reader are slim. This is why it is so important to learn as much as you can about effective methods of teaching vocabulary.

In this chapter, we have mentioned a number of current sources. We suggest you begin with Beck et al.'s (2002) *Bringing Words to Life: Robust Vocabulary Instruction*. This bestselling book describes many effective techniques, focusing especially on read-alouds. We also recommend a book edited by James Baumann and Edward Kame'enui (2004), *Vocabulary Instruction: Research to Practice*. Its contributors address a variety of issues related to vocabulary instruction, and they do so with insight and expertise. The most recent and comprehensive treatment is a book by Steven Stahl and William Nagy (2005), *Teaching Word Meanings*. This book provides clearly written background on what we know and do not know about vocabulary, then systematically reviews research-based approaches. Finally, two outstanding online sources are well worth a visit. One is housed on the University of Oregon's website: *reading.uoregon.edu/voc/voc_teach.php*. It focuses specifically on vocabulary instruction for beginning readers. The other source is an overview of research-based practice and is a part of *Put Reading First*, a free publication developed jointly by the Center for the Improvement of Early Reading Achievement (CIERA) and the National Institute for Literacy (NIFL): *www.nifl.gov/partnershipforreading/publications/reading_first1vocab.html*.

CHAPTER 7

Building Comprehension

The NRP's (National Institute of Child Health and Human Development, 2000) synthesis of research (*www.nationalreadingpanel.org/Publications/publications.htm*) included a chapter on the development of comprehension in classrooms. That report concluded that there are several approaches with some level of research support. The approaches with the strongest support were teaching comprehension monitoring, using graphic organizers, asking questions, teaching students to generate questions, and teaching summarization. Single-strategy approaches (focusing on one of these strategies in a lesson), multiple-strategy approaches (focusing on more than one in the same lesson), and cooperative learning approaches were all effective. In a separate chapter, the panel explored professional development models to support teachers' implementation of comprehension instruction. Two models (direct explanation and transactional strategies instruction) had research-based evidence of effectiveness. As in the work on vocabulary, few of the studies on comprehension instruction were conducted with young children.

RECENT RESEARCH AND REVIEWS

While the NRP report examines comprehension instruction as an independent component of reading instruction, this is only possible in the primary grades when text is read aloud by the teacher as a basis for listening comprehension. In the read-aloud event, comprehension and vocabulary can be the focus since the burden of word recognition is borne by the teacher. For novice and struggling readers, reading comprehension is related to vocabulary, just as it is for older readers, but it is also inextricably linked to decoding and fluency. That said, researchers continue to investigate the characteristics of effective comprehension instruction. Since the time of the NRP report, one research team (Kim, Vaughn, Wanzek, & Wei, 2004) has reviewed the existing research on using graphic organizers with students with LDs. They found 21 appropriate intervention studies, most of which used experimenter-designed measures of comprehension. On these measures, comprehension of specific texts by students with LDs improved significantly when they learned to use semantic organizers and cognitive maps and to take notes matching the structure of the text. These positive effects were found for high school students with LDs and for students with LDs in the upper elementary grades. There were insufficient data to make specific claims about the use of graphic organizers with children with LDs in the early elementary grades.

Another possible route to improving comprehension is teaching organizational patterns in different types of texts. Joanna Williams (2005) investigated the utility of text structure instruction for second- and third-grade students at risk for reading failure. In a series of studies, teachers were successful in boosting children's understanding of theme in narratives and compare-and-contrast organizational structures in information texts. She recommends highly structured instruction in text elements for elementary students.

Reutzel, Smith, and Fawson (2005) investigated the question of whether a single-strategy or a multiple-strategy approach was more effective with second graders reading science information texts. Both approaches used a gradual-release-of-responsibility model, in which the responsibility for comprehending slowly shifts from teacher to child. In the single-strategy approach, each of six strategies was taught for 2.5 weeks. In the multiple-strategy approach, eight strategies were introduced during the first month's instruction, and then all eight were gradually released to the children to choose and use during reading. The researchers found no difference on normative measures of comprehension, but the multiple-strategy group outperformed the single-strategy group on curriculum-based criterion-referenced measures. In addition, the two groups were similar in main-idea recall, but the multiple-strategy group outperformed the single-strategy group in the inclusion of details in their retellings of science information texts. Finally, the multiple-strategy group outperformed the single-strategy group in a science knowledge test. These results suggest that it may be wise to combine strategy instruction as appropriate to a particular text.

John Guthrie and his colleagues (Guthrie et al., 2004) extended the findings of the NRP by developing and testing an integrated approach to fostering comprehension and engagement. This approach they call concept-oriented reading instruction (CORI). CORI includes strategy instruction but nests that instruction within a larger framework designed to enhance engagement and develop science knowledge. The approach was used in third-grade units designed to teach life science. Students were motivated through the use of choice in texts and tasks, integrated hands-on activities, the use of science trade books, and collaborative activities. They were also taught the comprehension strategies of activating background knowledge, questioning, searching for information, summarizing, organizing graphically, and identifying story structure. Third-grade CORI students outperformed students who had comprehension strategy instruction without the additional motivation components as well as students experiencing traditional instruction in measures of specific passage comprehension, in standardized comprehension measures, in measures of motivation, and in measures of strategy use.

This study and others like it are beginning to fill gaps in what we know about comprehension instruction for primary-grade students. The principal lesson is that young children are capable of learning key strategies under the right instructional conditions. It is pointless, and risky as well, to put off teaching comprehension strategies until the upper elementary grades.

FOUNDATIONAL TEACHER KNOWLEDGE

Without a doubt, comprehension instruction is the most complex part of the elementary school curriculum. For comprehension instruction to be successful, teachers must adopt a gradual-release-of-responsibility model which we have illustrated in Figure 7.1. In that model, instruction begins with high levels of teacher control, moves to shared control, with teachers and students constructing meaning together, and finally progresses to high levels of individual student control, with students independently applying comprehension skills and strategies to understand new text.

For each new skill or strategy, the gradual-release model may take months to be fully realized. This is because independent application of specific cognitive strategies in reading is very complex for young learners. We recommend that teachers begin the process by modeling strategy use during read-alouds.

Modeling comprehension before, during, and after reading is itself very complex. There are several secrets to modeling well. First, the teacher must have a clear notion of the cognitive procedures involved in implementing a specific strategy. Next, the teacher must choose a time for modeling where that strategy is actually useful. Finally, the teacher must be able to explain the strategy in ways that

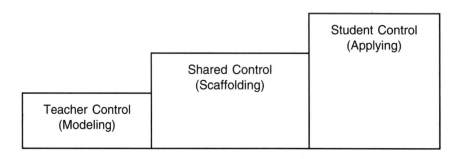

FIGURE 7.1. Gradual release of responsibility.

are accessible to students. Figure 7.2 (pp. 108–109) draws on the work of Gerald Duffy (2003) to provide sample teacher talk for strategies likely to be useful in the early grades.

One strategy that teachers commonly use both to support and to assess comprehension is asking questions. Not all questions, however, are created equal. Eileen Kintsch (2005) prepared a set of guidelines for the design of questions. She specifically targeted the types and goals of questions. We summarize them in Figure 7.3. She recommends that teachers ask questions of all three types, to elicit all three types of thinking when needed. If a reader can generate a summary or inference, then text-based questions are not really needed, but if the reader cannot construct meaning, then text-based questions can help him or her search for the information needed to summarize and to make inferences. The questions in Figure 7.4 would be useful in many different contexts and they may help you to include various types of questions as you support student understanding.

Type	Processing required
Text-based	Search of memory or search of the text
Summary	Construction of meaning from memory or from review of the text
Inference	Construction of connections between ideas, construction of analogies, application of text ideas to new situations

FIGURE 7.3. Types and goals of questions. Based on Kintsch (2005).

	Information text	Narrative
Summary questions	What is the most important information so far? Give me a summary of the most important parts of the section on _____.	What are the most important details so far? What were the main events in this chapter/part? How did the chapter/story end?
Inference questions	Describe some additional examples of that idea. Explain why these things are similar. What would happen if . . . ?	Describe the feelings of the characters at the end of the story. Why did they feel that way?

FIGURE 7.4. Questions that could be used in a variety of texts.

Strategy	Procedural knowledge	Sample teacher talk
Predicting	1. Look for clues in the words and pictures. 2. Think about what they already know about the topic. 3. On the basis of prior knowledge, predict what they think will happen.	Good readers predict before and during reading. Here I see a picture of a _____. I know that _____. Because of both what I see and what I know, I predict that this story will be about _____.
Monitoring, questioning, and repredicting	1. Keep the original prediction in mind. 2. Keep asking whether that prediction continues to make sense in light of new information from the text. 3. Use new information in the text and prior knowledge about that information to make new predictions.	I predicted that _____. So far, that might be right because the text says _____. I predicted that _____. That must not be true because the text says _____. My new prediction is _____.
Visualizing	1. Identify descriptive words the author is using. 2. Use prior knowledge about those words and about the world to create a visual image.	Good readers make pictures in their minds to help them to understand. I know that this story takes place _____. I know that setting would have _____. The author uses the words _____ and _____. In my mind I am visualizing _____.
Inferring	1. Note the clues embedded in the text. 2. Access their own experience regarding the clues. 3. Make inferences about the implied meaning based on experience and the clues the author provides.	The author tells us that this character is _____. Because of my own experience, I know that _____. Therefore, I think the character is _____.

(continued)

FIGURE 7.2. Comprehension strategy explanations.

Strategy	Procedural knowledge	Sample teacher talk
Using fix-up strategies	1. Stop when the text stops making sense. 2. Identify what is blocking meaning. 3. Think about what strategy they know that could be used to fix the problem. 4. Apply the strategy. 5. Test to see if the problem is fixed.	Wait. I thought that the text said _____. Here it says that _____. That doesn't make sense to me. I need to read ahead and see if the author tells me how both _____ and _____ could be true.
Finding the main idea	1. Put yourself in the author's place. 2. Examine words and phrases for clues to what is important to the author. 3. Ask questions about what, in their experience, the clues combined seem to say about what the author values.	The author has given me a whole lot of facts about _____ and about _____. Some of them are the same and some are different. I think that the main idea here is that _____ are similar to _____ in some ways and different in other ways.
Retelling a story	1. Know the parts of a story. 2. Review the book to identify the story information provided at the beginning, in the middle, and at the end.	I can use what I know about stories to retell this one very simply. I don't tell everything. I think about what the author usually does in the beginning, the middle, and the end. This story is set _____. The main characters are _____. The problem in the story is _____. The characters solve the problem by _____.
Synthesizing	1. Think about the content of each text. 2. Decide how they are alike and different. 3. Use experience about the common elements to create a synthesis.	When I want to think about two stories at once, I have to decide how they are alike and different. I first think about how they were alike. Our stories were alike because _____. Then I think about how they were different. Our stories were different because _____. Together, then, I can synthesize information from the stories to say that _____.

FIGURE 7.2. *(page 2 of 2)*

We present a series of strategies below that you can use in differentiated instruction for small groups. As in previous chapters, we think that such instruction is best when it is both targeted to individual needs and connected to the rest of your curriculum.

QUESTION CLUSTERS

Kintsch's notion of question "levels" actually has a long tradition (see, for example, Trabasso, van den Brock, & Lui, 1988), and one of the important lessons for teachers is that they can alter the levels of the questions they ask in order to model a thinking process. The result is a cluster of questions that fits seamlessly into a small-group discussion. Such a cluster has one goal—to reach a higher level of comprehension, such as an inference. However, there are two very different clusters of questions useful in attaining this goal.

A bottom-up cluster begins with one or more text-based questions and concludes with an inferential question. Such a cluster starts easy. The children are led by the teacher through questions that are readily answerable from the text. But the real agenda is a higher-level question that builds on the simpler, explicit questions.

A top-down cluster reverses the order of questions. The teacher begins by asking the upper-level question, calling for an inference. If the children cannot answer adequately, the teacher might "drop down" to one or more text-based questions. In a top-down cluster, the teacher wants to demonstrate how explicitly stated facts can be used to answer higher-level questions. Once the simpler questions have been posed, and the answers injected into the discussion, the teacher returns to the original question, which will now be much easier to answer.

What Kind of Reader Will Question Clusters Help?

Question clusters will assist readers who have yet to develop adequate proficiency at monitoring their own comprehension. These are children who, at best, read to glean superficial information but are not in the habit of integrating or reflecting on this information.

What Is the Instructional Focus of Question Clusters?

Question clusters provide children with gentle modeling of how proficient readers process text. Over a period of time, the goal is to make this strategic processing habitual. Children will eventually realize that text-based comprehension is inadequate, and in fact not true reading at all. Like all habits, however, this one is difficult to break, and in using question clusters teachers must be both persistent and consistent.

Where Do Question Clusters Come from?

The use of question clusters originated in the seminal volume *Teaching Reading Comprehension* (Pearson & Johnson, 1978). Question clusters help readers to see that meaning is built in their head rather than found in the text.

What Materials Are Needed for Question Clusters?

No materials are needed for this strategy other than a text that has just been read (or heard) by the needs-based group. Because question clusters are naturally nested within a larger discussion of the selection, no props, markers, equipment, or materials are required.

How Do You Prepare for Question Clusters?

Begin by carefully reading the selection, introspecting about your own comprehension as you do so. As proficient readers, teachers are sometimes unconscious of their own thought processes, but question clustering requires that you attend to exactly how you comprehend the selection. Be particularly alert to places where explicit facts are sufficient to support inferences that are not mentioned by the author. Jot down the explicit questions that support the inference. Then decide whether to ask them as part of a top-down or bottom-up cluster.

Figure 7.5 presents a short text about a boy and girl playing marbles. It is followed by two question clusters, one of each kind, focusing on the same inference. Note that the order of questions is the main difference. Top-down clusters are mainly for troubleshooting or for modeling the importance of supporting an inference to other children who might not have reached it. Bottom-up clusters are more basic and take nothing for granted. They lead children "by the nose" to a particular conclusion. For many struggling readers, this will be the place to start. These examples may help you better understand what clustering requires—and just how easy it is!

You will note that our sample passage is essentially a math word problem. We chose it to illustrate that all word problems involve bottom-up reasoning, in which the student uses available facts to infer a missing one. However, even this simple "math" passage can be used to take children in a different direction. Consider the following top-down cluster:

TEACHER: Do you think Ken will ask Julie to play marbles again?

CHILD: I don't know.

TEACHER: Well, what did it say about boys playing better than girls?

CHILD: That's what Ken thought?

TEACHER: And what happened?

CHILD: He lost.

TEACHER: Yes, and so do you think he will ask her to play again?

This cluster also illustrates that some inferences, such as predictions, are speculative. We simply can't be sure if we're right because we don't have enough facts. It's not a matter of subtracting marbles. Children must come to realize this and to arrive at inferences that are consistent with the facts but that may not be "iron clad." This kind of inferential reasoning is an integral part of proficient reading, and question clusters can signal that it is appropriate.

Finally, you must be prepared to explain your thinking process. This can amount to a mere reminder. In the example, the teacher might follow up by saying that even though the answer is not given, the children still have enough facts to answer it. They should look for chances to use the facts they read to come up with more facts. This message needs to be repeated—briefly and subtly, to be sure, but frequently.

Ken asked Julie to play marbles after school one day. Ken knew that boys are better than girls, and he knew he would win. Ken started with 25 marbles. When the match was over, he had 12.

Bottom-up cluster:

TEACHER: How many marbles did Ken have in the beginning?

CHILD: 25.

TEACHER: How many did he have afterward?

CHILD: 12.

TEACHER: How many marbles did Ken lose?

Top-down cluster:

TEACHER: How many marbles did Ken lose?

CHILD: It doesn't say.

TEACHER: Hmm, well let's see what it does say. How many marbles did Ken have in the beginning?

CHILD: 25.

TEACHER: And how many did he have afterward?

CHILD: 12.

TEACHER: So, even though it doesn't say, can you figure out how many marbles he lost?

FIGURE 7.5. Examples of top-down and bottom-up question clusters.

How Do You Implement Question Clusters?

In a read-aloud session, it is advisable to pause at a key point in order to ask the cluster of questions. This is because waiting until the end might make it difficult for children to recall the explicit facts. If the children have read the text already, perhaps as a core selection discussed in a whole-class setting, you can have them return to the pertinent portion as you ask the cluster of questions.

If you have decided on a top-down cluster and the child answers the inferential question correctly, you may still want to follow up so that other children are exposed to the ground-up thought process that led to the inference. An alternative is to deliver a brief think-aloud about the process. After Nacole correctly gives the number of marbles Ken lost, you might say, "That's right, Nacole. We read that he started with 25 and ended with 12. Even though the author doesn't tell us, we can subtract 12 from 25 ourselves and find that he must have lost 13."

A bottom-up cluster is a bit more straightforward in that the chances of a correct answer are higher. This is because you have "spoon fed" relevant facts to the children in the small group by asking them one or more text-based questions. This is all the more reason to conclude the cluster with a brief reminder that you have used facts that you have read to figure out another fact that the author did not provide.

How Do You Know If Question Clusters Are Working?

As children grow more comfortable with using explicitly stated facts to generate inferences, they will be able to explain how they arrived at them. For instance, the teacher might have asked Nacole how she knew that Ken had 13 marbles left even though this fact was not explicit. A second way of determining whether children are grasping the thinking process involved is simply by noting their success in answering the inferential questions, both in top-down and bottom-up settings.

QUESTION–ANSWER RELATIONSHIPS

Question–answer relationships (QARs) are closely connected with question clusters in that they allow teachers to capitalize on questions at more than one level of comprehension. QARs essentially take the matter a step further, however, by letting students know that there *are* more than one level. Implementing QARs involves directly teaching children about these levels, using child-friendly terminology to describe the thought processes required to answer each type.

...d of Reader Will QAR Help?

...gy is useful for novice readers or struggling comprehenders who are ...iculty drawing inferences during listening or reading. These children do not understand why or how readers "read between the lines," and tend to answer all questions with facts extracted directly from the text. They score poorly on measures of inferential comprehension.

What Is the Instructional Focus of QAR?

This is a comprehension strategy; it will not build fluency, vocabulary, or word recognition. The focus of this strategy is on defining and using four types of questions: Right There (explicit), Think and Search (making inferences across sentences in the text), Author and You (making inferences between the text and prior knowledge), and On Your Own (making personal responses to themes in the text).

Where Does QAR Come from?

This strategy (in fact, like most comprehension strategies) was developed and tested in the 1980s (Raphael, 1986). However, QARs have been especially long-lived, and have occasioned many extensions and reapplications since the original research. QARs are often part of comprehensive instructional materials.

What Materials Are Needed for QAR?

Teachers typically make a chart to introduce and define the four types of questions. Figure 7.6 presents an example of a QAR chart. The sample questions are based on the passage in Figure 7.5. Then you must select short texts to introduce the strategy. Once the children understand the types of questions and the concept of QARs, you can apply the strategy in virtually any text.

Right There	Think and Search
How many marbles did Ken have before he played Julie?	How many marbles did Ken lose to Julie?
Author and You	**On Your Own**
Have you ever lost more marbles than Ken?	If you were Ken, would you invite Julie to play again?

FIGURE 7.6. Example of a QAR chart based on the passage in Figure 7.5.

How Do You Prepare for QAR?

When you are first teaching the strategy, you need to use a short text with several questions and answers of each type already prepared. That text is used to teach the concepts of the four types of questions. After that, preparing questions of each type before instruction ensures that the strategy can be employed quickly during needs-based instruction. We actually find it very difficult to construct questions of all types "on the fly," so it is advisable to write the questions in advance. Typically, if you begin with the inferences (the Think and Search questions) you know what to target in the other questions. If teachers are working together to implement QAR, then they can keep the questions constructed for specific books to shorten preparation time.

How Do You Implement QAR?

At first, the strategy is taught by having children identify the relationship between specific questions and answers. Once they understand that concept, the strategy can be employed during and after reading narrative and information text. Teachers can ask questions, telling children what type they are. Alternatively, they can ask questions, elicit answers, and then ask children to categorize the questions by type, essentially tracking their own thinking. Finally, teachers can ask children to generate questions of each type during and after reading.

How Do You Know If QAR Is Working?

You will know this strategy is working when children are able to categorize the four target relationships between questions and answers and when they are better able to recognize and use the relationships to answer or ask questions.

STORY MAPPING

Because most genres, from limericks to research reports to short stories, rely on structural formulas of some kind, it is a good idea to let students in on how these structures work. This knowledge helps them comprehend because they have a useful frame of reference for interpreting the text they encounter. Think of the structure as a blueprint and the actual text as bricks and mortar. One way of helping students gain a knowledge of structure focuses on the general structure of the short story. Teaching children the "blueprint" of a typical story has proved effective in improving comprehension, not only of a particular story but new stories children encounter in the future as well.

What Kind of Reader Will Story Mapping Help?

Story mapping instruction will help students who have difficulty generating an accurate retelling. After first grade, teachers can screen for narrative text structure knowledge by reading a text aloud and asking students to complete a written story map. Among the students who struggle with this mapping task, those who have adequate decoding skills would benefit from needs-based instruction in story mapping. This strategy could be combined with a fluency-building strategy.

What Is the Instructional Focus of Story Mapping?

Story mapping teaches students to focus attention on setting, characters, problem–solution–outcome, reaction, and theme to help them comprehend, remember, and retell narratives. Story mapping only works with narrative text with that specific structure. However, such texts comprise the bulk of narrative texts.

Where Does Story Mapping Come from?

Story mapping has a long history in research and practice. The version we are summarizing comes from a recent study (Boulineau, Fore, Hagan-Burke, & Burke, 2004) in which third- and fourth-grade students with LDs were taught to use story maps. The authors learned that such instruction was effective in increasing comprehension of stories and that the effects of the instruction persisted after the intervention.

What Materials Are Needed for Story Mapping?

For all comprehension modeling, a story map for modeling, on chart paper or on a transparency, helps students see the teacher's thinking during instruction. Such a map must be constructed so that it can be filled in during reading (rather than simply created, fully formed, in advance). After modeling, as students are working to apply the strategy in additional texts and contexts, they need their own version of the map. Figure 7.7 provides a template for such a map.

Beside the maps, you must find texts! Since you will be using these in small-group instruction, shorter selections are more useful. We suggest that you use brief narratives (either trade books or basal selections) with straightforward story structure.

How Do You Prepare for Story Mapping?

Prepare child-friendly descriptions of the parts of the narrative that you are targeting: setting/time, main characters, problem–solution–outcome, reaction, and

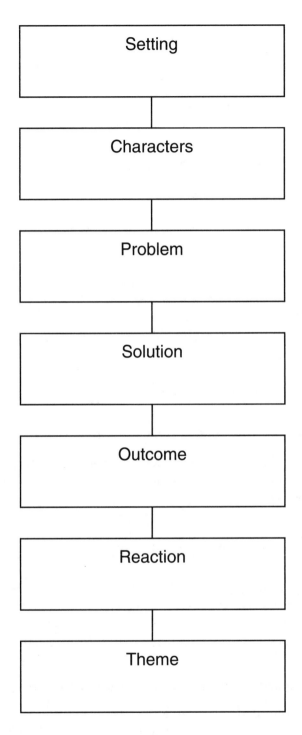

FIGURE 7.7. Template of a story map.

theme. Choose at least one text that you can read orally to model the procedure of story mapping. The procedure involves selection of important elements to include and to exclude during and after reading. Mark each text to be used so that you can stop student reading as each story element is revealed.

How Do You Implement Story Mapping?

Once you have introduced the strategy, each day:

1. Review the story map, reminding students that good readers use story maps to help them focus on and remember the most important parts of stories.
2. Have students whisper, read, or listen to the day's story, paying attention to the story map features. If students need to build fluency, ask them to read it repeatedly or provide an assisted fluency support.
3. Ask students to read until the first story element is revealed.
4. Model or provide guided practice on identifying that element and writing it on the map.
5. Continue until the story is completed.

How Do You Know If Story Mapping Is Working?

After several sessions of story mapping with teacher support for fluency and comprehension, ask students to read or listen to a new story and comprehend its story structure independently.

TEXT STRUCTURE INSTRUCTION

Just as story maps provide children with a blueprint to help them interpret fiction, similar strategies have been developed for nonfiction. One of the best-researched approaches targets expository texts that compare or contrast concepts. It has proved to be especially effective with students in grades 2 and 3.

What Kind of Reader Will Text Structure Instruction Help?

This strategy is designed for a third-grade reader who has strong decoding and fluency skills but struggles with comprehension. Such a reader will have adequate oral reading fluency scores but might do poorly on a criterion-referenced or normative comprehension measure. This strategy would also be appropriate for a second-grade student with little exposure to the structure of expository text.

What Is the Instructional Focus of Text Structure Instruction?

This lesson focuses on recognition of compare–contrast structures in expository text, one of the six most common expository text structures. (Others include description, chronological sequence, explanation, definition and example, and problem–solution. Each of those structures is important to comprehension of expository text.)

Where Does Text Structure Instruction Come from?

This strategy was used by Joanna Williams (2005) in a series of studies with at-risk second- and third-grade students. The strategy is adapted here so that it can be applied to more texts.

What Materials Are Needed for Text Structure Instruction?

You will need to locate texts of appropriate difficulty that have compare–contrast structures. These might involve core selections or trade books. An example is *Spiders Are Not Insects*, by Allan Fowler (Children's Press, 1996). You will also need one or more graphic organizers to highlight compare–contrast structures. A Venn diagram or a two-column chart could be used. Also useful is a chart of clue words and phrases that signal compare and contrast. The five clue words used by Williams and her colleagues were: *both*, *alike*, *also*, *but*, and *however* (Stafford, Williams, Nubla-Kung, & Pollini, 2005). Other compare–contrast words include *than*, *contrast*, *on the other hand*, *similar*, and *compare*. Finally, it is helpful to have a chart of compare–contrast questions: What two things is this text about? How are they the same? How are they different?

How Do You Prepare for Text Structure Instruction?

Plan a brief prior knowledge and vocabulary lesson so that the students have background knowledge on each of the two concepts covered in the text. Be sure that the focus of the lesson is on how to understand a text that compares and contrasts two concepts rather than on initial learning of each concept.

How Do You Implement Text Structure Instruction?

Begin by building prior knowledge and discussing key vocabulary. Next, ask the students to read the new text silently. If your group is not sufficiently fluent, read the selection aloud while students track. After reading, lead a discussion to identify clue words and facts. Use your graphic organizer and compare–contrast questions. Based on the organizer, have the students write a summary paragraph. Finally, review the strategy for recognizing and using compare and contrast structures to understand text.

How Do You Know If Text Structure Instruction Is Working?

The only way to be sure this strategy is working is to arrange for a transfer task. When students gain proficiency with the strategy, give them a new compare–contrast text and ask them to write a summary paragraph without teacher scaffolding

DIRECT EXPLANATION

There are two schools of thought regarding the best way to foster comprehension strategies in young readers. The indirect approach involves modeling and reminding, embedding such instruction in the context of read-alouds and discussion. An example is question clustering. The direct approach makes comprehension strategies the focus of carefully planned explicit teaching, during which the teacher presents and "explains" each strategy directly, followed by opportunities to apply it. Both direct and indirect teaching have impressive research bases, and it is not necessary to decide between them. We turn now to direct explanation, an instructional technique that we think you will find works well in tandem with more indirect methods of teaching strategies.

What Kind of Reader Will Direct Explanation Help?

Direct explanation is aimed at providing a clear introduction to a comprehension strategy, demonstrating how it is used and why we should use it. During read-alouds, it can be a powerful tool for assisting novice readers without strong comprehension skills. It is also useful for older readers who are struggling with comprehension, and it is potentially useful beginning in kindergarten, as long as the strategies are explained and applied in appropriate language and contexts.

What Is the Instructional Focus of Direct Explanation?

The focus of direct explanation is making clear the procedural (how-to) knowledge that underlies the application of a strategy. The teacher uses a clear lesson introduction and then a think-aloud during reading to make the cognitive processes that good readers use transparent to novice or struggling readers.

Where Does Direct Explanation Come from?

Direct explanation was the focus of a series of comprehension studies in second grade in the 1980s. More recently, the principal author of those studies, Gerald Duffy, has released a professional book on explanation for a variety of strategies and skills: *Explaining Reading: A Resource for Teaching Concepts, Skills, and Strategies* (2003).

What Materials Are Needed for Direct Explanation?

You will need a clear definition of the strategy you will explain, including the procedures it entails. A good source of such information is your core program. You will also need texts to use to model the strategy and for children to practice applying it. There is no real constraint on which texts to select since every high-quality text provides a context for strategy use. Make sure, however, that the texts you select are at or near the children's instructional level if they are early readers or near their listening level if they are beginning readers and you will be reading the text aloud. Also, beware of teaching children to apply a specific strategy in a particular text that is not a good match—strategy instruction, if it is to be successful, demands that students see that the work required in implementing a particular strategy is worthwhile in that it yields improved comprehension.

How Do You Prepare for Direct Explanation?

The most challenging aspect of teaching comprehension strategies is knowing which strategy to teach in a particular text. We recommend that teachers begin by writing strategy introductions for all of the strategies that they will teach over the course of the school year. Then, as they are reading a new text aloud to the whole class or in a needs-based group, they can flexibly choose among the strategies they have prepared to teach. Check your core reading materials to see if such strategy introductions are already available to you. Remember, too, that once you have directly explained a given strategy, you cannot expect your struggling readers to fully internalize it. Be prepared to return many times to your explanation in order to freshen memories.

How Do You Implement Direct Explanation?

Before reading, tell students clearly and directly what strategy they will learn to use that day and how it will help them to understand the text. Then tell the students the steps that are used to employ the strategy. Begin your read-aloud (or have the students begin reading). Stop reading at a point where modeling the strategy is natural and useful to comprehension. Think aloud as you apply the strategy. Continue to read. Repeat the modeling process several times. Then provide students opportunities to share their thinking and use of the strategy.

How Do You Know If Direct Explanation Is Working?

You will know that direct explanation is working when students can verbalize the cognitive procedures involved in the strategy and choose to use the strategy independently.

SUMMARIZATION

Teaching children to summarize has been identified by the NRP (National Institute of Child Health and Human Development, 2000) as a well-validated instructional strategy. And no wonder—a good summary requires the reader to make key decisions about importance and to create a mental overview of what has been read. This is not an easy proficiency to instill, but effective techniques have been developed in the recent past. We describe one of them.

What Kind of Reader Will Summarization Help?

Direct instruction in summarization will help older elementary students who are struggling to understand and remember when they read information text. Those children appear better able to retell completely than to summarize, and they are unlikely to do well on standardized measures of comprehension. Most of the work of this strategy is done in writing, so fluency with spelling is a prerequisite.

What Is the Instructional Focus of Summarization?

The focus of this strategy is strictly on building comprehension by writing summaries. It will not improve fluency, vocabulary, or word recognition.

Where Does Summarization Come from?

This instructional strategy was developed and tested with at-risk adolescents (Hare & Borchardt, 1984). We choose it because the summary rules are clear and can be applied as a strategy to texts appropriate for younger children. However, as you read about the procedure, be mindful of whether this particular strategy can be understood by the readers you teach.

What Materials Are Needed for Summarization?

You will need a chart of the summarization procedures. The chart will be used to review the process with children and to serve as a reference as they write their own summaries. You will also need several short information texts that you can use in modeling the procedure. Finally, you will need a set of texts for scaffolding children and to give them opportunities to independently apply the technique.

How Do You Prepare for Summarization?

There is very little teacher preparation needed to teach this strategy, but that does not mean that it is simple to teach. The real work of instruction takes place in response to student work, rather than in the preparation stage. After modeling, it may be possible to use the strategy with one text over several days, with students reading and discussing the text during needs-based instruction, and then writing their summaries during their independent practice time.

How Do You Implement Summarization?

Ask the students to read the text. Then model the use of this procedure, using a large chart that will remain in the room as a reference:

1. Make sure you understand the text.
2. Reread to check your understanding, marking important parts.
3. Rethink, making sure that you can say the main idea of each paragraph. Write the main idea as a note to yourself.
4. Write your summary, checking to make sure that you avoided lists, included or created topic sentences, got rid of unnecessary details, and combined paragraphs.
5. Check your summary and edit it so that it sounds natural.

How Do You Know If Summarization Is Working?

You will know if this strategy is working when students begin to generate more succinct summaries that exclude unimportant details, when they understand and can talk about the summary procedures, and when they can use the strategy without assistance.

TO LEARN MORE

Because comprehension is the only goal of reading, all teachers should learn as much as they can about how to foster it. Fortunately, extensive research has informed best practice in the last few years. We highly recommend three books that will help frame current thinking and give you much to digest. The first is *Comprehension Instruction: Research-Based Best Practices*, a wide-ranging collection of chapters edited by Cathy Collins Block and Michael Pressley (2002). The second is also a cutting-edge edited volume, *Rethinking Reading Comprehension*, compiled by Anne Sweet and Catherine Snow (2003). The last is a report commissioned by the RAND Reading Study Group (2002). Its authors define comprehension, summarize research, and point to future research agendas. This report is available free online at *www.rand.org/multi/achievementforall/reading/*.

Other online sources include the University of Oregon's website (*reading.uoregon.edu/comp/*) and a portion of *Put Reading First*, a free publication developed jointly by the Center for the Improvement of Early Reading Achievement (CIERA) and the National Institute for Literacy (NIFL): *www.nifl.gov/partnershipforreading/publications/reading_first1text.html*.

CHAPTER 8

A Kindergarten Differentiation Plan

Chapters 8, 9, 10, and 11 provide an illustration of the concepts that we have introduced in the context of kindergarten, first-grade, second-grade, and third-grade small-group differentiated instruction. We have constructed each example with a specific set of children, assessments, and curriculum resources in mind. Remember that our goal in this text is to support your thinking as your build your own differentiation plan; no one of these examples is likely to transfer directly to your classroom. The concepts, though, do travel!

Mrs. Coffey is an experienced kindergarten teacher, but she is using a new set of instructional materials for the first time. As she plans for differentiation, she carefully reviews the organization of her instructional materials and she reflects on student achievement data, both formal and informal. She has 2 hours to teach her literacy block, and those hours are protected from interruption. Her goal for differentiation is to plan for 1 hour of whole-group instruction, mostly geared toward developing comprehension and vocabulary, and then to plan for 1 hour of differentiated instruction, with three needs-based groups rotating as follows: (1) instruction with her, (2) one required follow-up activity, and (3) one choice center.

During the literacy block, Mrs. Coffey has created a listening comprehension center, where children listen to books on audiotape and then draw a picture of their favorite part of the story. She also has a word-work center, where children can choose among a variety of alphabet activities and games. Finally, she has a writing-for-sounds center, where children choose pictures from a large basket, then use dry-erase boards either to label the pictures or to write simple sentences about the pictures. Nine children (3 in each center) can work comfortably in centers; Mrs. Coffey's 19 children, then, can be divided again and again into three or four groups, and those groups can range in size, depending on the most current student achievement data.

STEP 1: GATHER RESOURCES

Mrs. Coffey first gathers and organizes her resources. Her centers are not new; she has a large collection of children's literature with audio versions for her comprehension center, and each year she adds new titles and rotates older titles from the school's library collection. Since she has a new core basal reading program, she has many new activities to place in her word-work center. She doesn't know exactly how to sequence those activities, though, so she turns her attention to the scope and sequence of her new program.

Curriculum Resources

The basal core program has many charts and guides, but Mrs. Coffey wants to really know the program's skeleton—its organizational structure. She quickly realizes that the activities are varied, and that there are many choices that she must make as she plans for instruction. Figure 8.1 is a sample of the chart that she

Decoding/spelling/ alphabet	High-frequency words	Comprehension skills/strategies
Cc	get	Predicting
Short i	where	Using illustrations
Dd	it	Story elements—plot, setting, and theme
Ll	the	Character
Short o	can	Recall and retell
Kk	is	Compare and contrast
	my	Summarizing
	do	Sequence
	up	
	red	
	one	
	what	
	here	
	three	
	little	
	two	

FIGURE 8.1. Kindergarten basal scope-and-sequence summary from one theme in a basal program.

makes for herself so that she can keep track of children's achievement in the program; it represents the most important content from one of the basal's themes. In terms of phonics, she makes special note of the fact that the program combines attention to phonemic awareness and phonics, introduces consonants in small sets in the initial position in many words, and also introduces short vowels both in the initial position and in short-vowel, one-syllable word families. For comprehension, she sees that the program has several useful story maps that she can move into her listening center. The high-frequency words that are introduced have a strong overlap with the ones that she taught last year, but they are in a different order. She knows that it will be better to redo her word wall from scratch rather than to add the new words to her existing list; she will add words to the wall as she teaches them.

Assessment Resources

Mrs. Coffey's district procedures include a norm-referenced screening test for vocabulary; all of her students, as part of kindergarten registration, will take the Peabody Picture Vocabulary Test, 3rd edition (PPVT-III). PPVT-III results will be used as outcome measures for language development and to select children for a language development intervention group that is designed by the speech-language pathologist at the school. The goal of that program is to accelerate oral language development for the neediest children at the onset of kindergarten; given the strength of these oral vocabulary data, Mrs. Coffey does not need to conduct additional assessments of vocabulary to guide her in making a differentiation plan; she also knows from experience that the PPVT-III scores reliably identify children whose comprehension is weak.

Next Mrs. Coffey looks for useful assessments that come with her core, especially in the areas of phonemic awareness and phonics. Here she is disappointed; she expects to find a phonemic awareness screening test and various measures of alphabet knowledge. Since these are not included in the program materials, she gathers assessments that will help provide screening data, be useful for grouping students, and provide direction to her differentiated, needs-based instruction time. She chooses among assessments presented in McKenna and Stahl's (2003) *Assessment for Reading Instruction*. Figure 8.2 presents her choices and her plans for using the assessments. She decides to use the same measures for screening, diagnosis, and progress monitoring because the tools she has chosen are so flexible.

Finally, she makes two additional assessments. The first is a sight-word inventory matched to the scope and sequence of sight words in her core program. She will administer this progress monitoring tool to all of her children at the end of each theme so that she can reteach words that children have trouble with. The first portion of this inventory appears in Figure 8.3. You will note that it presents only those words that will be introduced in the theme (see Figure 8.1). These words are

Tool	Purpose
Letter-name inventory	Screening, diagnosis, progress monitoring
Letter-sound inventory	Screening, diagnosis, progress monitory
Phonemic segmentation test	Screening, diagnosis, progress monitoring
Developmental spelling test	Screening, diagnosis, progress monitoring

FIGURE 8.2. Assessment plan for Mrs. Coffey's kindergarten class.

shown in isolation and the child is asked to pronounce each one. Mrs. Coffey uses an identical copy to note which words the child cannot identify at sight. She uses note cards to reveal one word at a time and is mindful of how long it takes to respond. A sight word can be pronounced in no more than a second. She marks each word with a checkmark if it is known by sight, with a *D* if it is decoded accurately after more than about a second, or with a *DK* if the child does not know the word.

Next, she makes a letter-name and letter-sound inventory, again matched to the scope and sequence of alphabet instruction in her core. The letter-name inventory simply presents all of the letters that will be introduced in a given theme (in this case, *c*, *d*, *l*, and *k*). The letters are displayed in isolation and in random order. She includes both upper and lower cases, except for *c* and *k*, which have nearly identical upper- and lower-case forms. The beginning of her inventory—the portion corresponding to the first theme of the basal—appears in Figure 8.4. One copy is shown to the child while Mrs. Coffey uses a second copy to record letters that the child cannot yet recognize. The letter-sound inventory, presented in Figure 8.5, simply lists the letters that will be presented in the theme as part of phonics study. This time the directions to the child are to say not the letter *name* but the *sound* the letter makes. Since both inventories require spoken responses, both must be given individually, but they are typically quick to administer and yield re-

get	can	up	here
where	is	red	three
it	my	one	little
the	do	what	two

FIGURE 8.3. Sight-word inventory for one kindergarten theme.

L   c   D   k   d   l

FIGURE 8.4. Letter-name inventory for one kindergarten theme.

sults that immediately help with instructional planning. Mrs. Coffey makes a new inventory for each theme and then strings them together, administering only the part corresponding to each theme. She will administer these inventories again at the end of each theme so that she can reflect on the effectiveness of her instruction and adapt it to the growing skills of her children.

STEP 2: CONSIDER YOUR CHILDREN'S NEEDS

Mrs. Coffey's experience tells her that she will have a very wide range of achievement in her classroom at the start of the year. A few of her kindergarteners will already be reading and writing conventionally, but a few will have almost no alphabet knowledge. She wants to begin to teach her children to work in small groups and in her centers beginning in the second week of school, so her plan is to make her first set of groups based solely on the results of her letter-name and letter-sound inventories. She will give the letter-name inventory to all of the students, and then she will give the letter-sound inventory to students who know at least half of the letter names. She knows that these groupings will be imperfect, but she also knows that they will allow her to begin differentiated instruction very quickly.

Instructional Groups Based on the Data

Mrs. Coffey will use a simple chart to summarize the letter-name and letter-sound data for her class. She anticipates one group with virtually no letter-name knowledge; she anticipates one group with strong knowledge of both letter names and letter sounds. She anticipates that most of her children will fall somewhere in between—they may know many letter names, and a few letter sounds, but the ones that they need to learn will not be consistent. She also knows that she will be able to teach many of the letter names and sounds in the course of her whole-group instruction and many of her children will learn their alphabet easily once regular instruction begins.

o   c   l   i   d   k

FIGURE 8.5. Letter-sound inventory for one kindergarten theme. (Ask the child for both hard and soft *c*: "Can you think of another sound this letter makes?")

As the year progresses, Mrs. Coffey's instructional groups and her instructional focus will shift and become more precise. After the first 4 weeks of instruction, she will use the next segment of her screening tools–the letter-name, letter-sound, and high-frequency word inventories she has made to match her instruction. After 12 weeks of instruction, she will administer the spelling inventory, again providing feedback for her groupings and focus for her differentiation.

Areas to Target for Each Group

Mrs. Coffey relies on her knowledge of kindergarten reading development to anticipate that she will spend at least the first half of the year focusing on differentiating for phonemic awareness and word recognition for all three of her instructional groups. Her goal is that all of her students will leave kindergarten with a firm grasp of the alphabetic principle and its application in decoding and spelling unknown words. Because of this, all of her students will read and spell words every day in their small-group instruction.

Differentiation Strategies in Those Areas

Mrs. Coffey will use simple and repetitive instructional strategies to provide differentiation for her kindergarteners; what will change over time and between groups is the content that she is teaching. In the area of phonemic awareness, she will begin the year with two strategies: initial sound sorting and say-it-and-move-it. See Chapter 3 for a review of these strategies. In the area of word recognition, she will teach letter names and sounds, sounding and blending, and high-frequency words. You will recall that they are described in Chapter 4.

Mrs. Coffey is not providing a balanced diet during her differentiated time; nevertheless, she *is* providing a balanced diet if you look across the whole-group and small-group instruction in which all children engage each day. Figure 8.6 presents the strategies and focus for her whole-group instruction, and Figure 8.7 is a conceptual plan for her differentiated instruction for each of three potential groups. You will notice that group 1, the group with the weakest letter-name and letter-sound knowledge, will engage in a larger variety of activities. In fact, they might also spend a slightly longer period of time in this portion of their instructional day. To make her management plan consistent even though her small-group time might be slightly varied for each group, she uses a chime to signal transitions between activities. Her students learn that when they hear the chime, they have 3 minutes to put away materials from their current activity and to move to their next one.

Goal	Materials	Daily activities
• Development of alphabetic principle • Development of phonemic awareness • Development of alphabet knowledge • Development of oral vocabulary	• Core program alphabet manipulatives • Core program big books • Trade books	• Alphabet and rhyming songs • Explicit letter-name and letter-sound instruction • High-frequency word instruction • Shared reading • Choral fingerpoint reading • Interactive read-alouds with modeling • Explicit vocabulary instruction • Interactive writing

FIGURE 8.6. A big-picture plan for kindergarten whole-group instruction.

Group 1	Group 2	Group 3
• Phonemic awareness and phonics • Alphabet tracking • Initial sound sorting • Letter names and sounds • Sounding and blending	• Phonemic awareness and phonics • Say-it-and-move-it • Sounding and blending • High-frequency words	• Phonics and word recognition • Sounding and blending • High-frequency words
Independent extension	Independent extension	Independent extension
Children will work on a specific alphabet activity each day.	Children will write for sounds from a specific prompt each day.	Children will write for sounds from a specific prompt each day.
Small-group center	Small-group center	Small-group center
Children will choose among three small-group centers each day (writing for sounds, word work, listening comprehension), but they must work in each center at least once a week.	Children will choose among three small-group centers each day (writing for sounds, word work, listening comprehension), but they must work in each center at least once a week.	Children will choose among three small-group centers each day (writing for sounds, word work, listening comprehension), but they must work in each center at least once a week.

FIGURE 8.7. A big-picture plan for kindergarten small-group differentiated instruction.

STEP 3: PLAN FOR 3 WEEKS OF INSTRUCTION

Mrs. Coffey knows that the only way to make good use of her instructional time is to have her materials organized and stored for easy access. At her small-group table, she has a set of dry-erase boards, markers, and felt erasers, a large pocket chart for modeling, an easel, and sets of teacher and student manipulatives: letters, picture cards, word cards, say-it-and-move-it boards, and bingo chips. Each place at the table has an individual alphabet strip fastened to the table with clear tape. On the Friday before a new 3-week series of differentiated instruction, she organizes all of her materials so that she can model and students can engage in guided practice during differentiated time. For initial sound sorting, she organizes her picture cards to review the sounds that she has taught in whole-group instruction and to preview the current sounds. For letter names and sounds, she organizes her own large letter cards for modeling and then she makes sets of individual ones for each child. Again, these are chosen to review previously taught letters and sounds and to preview upcoming ones so that her struggling readers will be more likely to be able to learn them during whole-group instruction. Sounding and blending instruction also constitutes review of sounds and patterns that have been taught previously, and she is careful to use the scope and sequence from the core to guide her thinking, but also to remember that some children will need many more examples. She prepares lists of words in advance that have the phonic elements that she is targeting. As she prepares those materials, she considers the needs of group 1. As these children master individual skills, she will increase her pace and present more challenging work.

For group 2, where Mrs. Coffey will also use say-it-and-move-it and work with high-frequency words, she plans to use these strategies to help the children develop deep understanding of the structure of both the individual words and the patterns that she is teaching during whole-group instruction. Again, she begins with the scope and sequence of her core and makes lists of additional examples. She hopes to move quickly from oral tasks to having the students spell the words during these activities.

Group 3 is likely to need less time for practice with these skills, but Mrs. Coffey wants to be sure that these children learn to apply their word recognition strategies and their phonics skills to unknown words. Again, the trick is having a longer list of examples, especially examples that have the same patterns as those taught in whole group, but that constitute new applications.

Finally, Mrs. Coffey knows that small-group time for vocabulary and comprehension development will benefit all three of her groups. Once each week, she uses her small-group time to revisit the whole-group read-aloud. During this time, she reviews the vocabulary words and the comprehension strategies that she has taught, and she gives each of the children, in each of the groups, a chance to participate in a scaffolded retelling.

STEP 4: PLAN FOR REFLECTION

Mrs. Coffey engages in reflection about her teaching and about her students' learning as they grow and change. She uses screenings several times each year to check progress; she regroups her children for small-group, differentiated instruction as often as individual progress warrants it, and she constantly evaluates whether the plans she has made are sufficiently challenging to engage all of her children in real learning during their needs-based instruction.

CHAPTER 9

A First-Grade Differentiation Plan

Mr. Hartline has a difficult assignment. As in many urban districts, mobility of teachers and students is very high, and district administrators often must make changes in individual teaching assignments during the course of an academic year. He is coming into a new classroom at midyear because the original classroom teacher has been battling health problems all year and finally has gone on extended sick leave. Consequently, children in the classroom have had many disruptions to their instruction.

Mr. Hartline is a career changer; although he is in his mid-40s, he is only a second-year teacher. He has spent his first 2 years teaching second grade, so he has a strong understanding of what the second-grade portion of the core curriculum demands in terms of student skills and strategies; he does not know the first-grade curriculum. He has had strong district-level mentoring, and he has excellent organizational and classroom management skills. He is determined to make the best of the remaining instructional days, and in order to do that he knows that his differentiated instruction must be diagnostically focused.

STEP 1: GATHER RESOURCES

As Mr. Hartline moves into a new classroom, he first simplifies the physical environment. He removes all items and decorations from the classroom that are not absolutely necessary for teaching and learning. He creates space on the classroom walls to display student work, to display content from current lessons, and to post daily schedules and agendas. He makes clear spaces for small-group instruction, for whole-group instruction, and for independent work.

Curriculum Resources

Mr. Hartline reviews the scope and sequence of the core program that he has to work with; he notices immediately that the decoding demands on the children are very high. His notes for the upcoming unit are provided in Figure 9.1; he will make similar notes for each unit. The program uses a synthetic phonics approach—children are taught to look at the letters in the word and make the individual sounds in sequence, blending them together to make words. Individual sounds are taught in various positions (at the beginning, middle, and end of words), and different spellings are taught for the same sound. Oral vocabulary is taught directly for stories from the anthology; many words are defined in each selection. Comprehension strategies, too, are taught during read-alouds of core selections, and there is explicit support for teacher modeling before and during reading and for comprehension-building discussions after reading. Mr. Hartline thinks

Decoding/spelling/ alphabet	High-frequency words	Comprehension skills/strategies
/k/	been	Monitoring and clarifying
/ng/	very	Predicting
/kw/	could	Classifying and categorizing
/y/	go	Visualizing
Long *a, a__e*	live	Summarizing
/s/, *ce, ci*	over	Main ideas and details
Long *i, i__e*	around	Asking questions
Long *o, o__e*	eating	Making connections
/v/	look	Drawing conclusions
Long *u, u__*	saw	
	some	
	together	
	give	
	use	
	please	
	once	
	read	
	goes	
	again	
	today	

FIGURE 9.1. First-grade basal scope-and-sequence summary.

that he can understand and use the vocabulary and comprehension portions of the lessons to good effect; in fact, the program teaches the same comprehension strategies in both first and second grade. There are genre-based graphic organizers, sound–symbol cards, and both decoding and comprehension strategy procedures that are used in many different ways and that he can post in the room as resources for children. However, Mr. Hartline knows that the success of his work with the word recognition instruction portion of the program will depend, to a large extent, on the match between the skills of his children and the demands of the curriculum. He also knows, firsthand, how difficult the second-grade curriculum is for those students who leave first grade without successful beginning reading experiences.

Assessment Resources

Curriculum-specific assessments would be especially helpful here, and he does locate some useful tools. The basal series has a word recognition test that assesses mastery of high-frequency words taught in the previous unit; he can use that. He is curious about oral reading fluency, but there are no fluency monitors provided with the program. He is also aware that his review of the materials indicates that success at this point in the year demands high levels of phonics knowledge; he may need to use a phonics inventory to investigate his students' proficiency.

Mr. Hartline needs to begin by screening his entire group, and then use informal diagnostic tests for those children whose screening scores indicate that there might be a problem. He knows that first graders are often not automatic enough in their decoding to make reading comprehension screenings valuable; he decides that oral reading fluency scores will be more useful under the circumstances. Figure 9.2 is a summary of his assessment strategy. Since he is planning for instruction immediately, he chooses the upcoming passage in the basal series to use for initial guidance in grouping and to direct further assessment.

Tool	Purpose
Upcoming anthology selection	Oral reading fluency screening
High-frequency word inventory	Diagnostic for students whose oral reading fluency is weak
Phonics inventory	Diagnostic for students whose oral reading fluency is weak

FIGURE 9.2. Assessment plan for Mr. Hartline's first-grade class.

STEP 2: CONSIDER YOUR CHILDREN'S NEEDS

Mr. Hartline has 21 children in his first-grade class. He must administer the oral reading passage to every one of those children, since he has chosen it as a screening tool. He is also very conscious of the need to get started with small-group differentiated instruction, so, all on the same day, he listens to each child in the class read the fluency passage aloud without support, calculating the number of words correct in 1 minute. Even considering transition and set-up time, the screening process is actually quite brief. He notices immediately that a portion of the class can read the passage with high levels of accuracy and with relatively little difficulty; most of the class, however, is struggling, some with scores of fewer than 10 words correct in 1 minute.

For the students who are struggling, Mr. Hartline has to consider two potential general explanations: they may be struggling with reading fluency, or they may be struggling with word recognition (a more basic proficiency and a prerequisite of fluency). On the very next day, Mr. Hartline administers two informal diagnostic tools to those children who scored poorly on the oral reading passage: the high-frequency word inventory that he found with the program, and a phonics inventory that he had used in his previous school. The phonics inventory assesses consonant sounds, short-vowel word families, vowel–consonant–*e* patterns, *r*-controlled patterns, and vowel teams. Given the instruction that is upcoming in the core scope and sequence, students would need to score very well on all individual consonant sounds and on short-vowel word families; the next unit teaches vowel–consonant–*e*.

Now that Mr. Hartline has reviewed his core materials and gathered some data to guide his differentiation, he expects that he will need to spend much of his time and attention on small-group, differentiated instruction. He anticipates that some of his children will also require intensive intervention, in addition to the differentiated instruction that he will provide during his language arts block, in order to leave first grade with adequate achievement. From the start, Mr. Hartline anticipates that the district-mandated 90-minute instructional block will be insufficient; he extends his block to 2 hours by adjusting his classroom schedule without disrupting his interaction with other teachers.

Instructional Groups Based on the Data

Mr. Hartline is faced with a classic problem. He has one group of students who scored well on his oral reading fluency screening. For the remaining students, he has two scores—the high-frequency word inventory score and the phonics inventory score. He decides to teach high-frequency words to both groups, so he uses the phonics screening measure to make two distinct groups—children who have not yet mastered all of their consonant sounds and thus are struggling with very basic decoding, and children who know their consonant sounds but are not working effectively with short vowels. Given that the core scope and sequence (see Figure 9.1) indicates that upcoming lessons will teach two different long-vowel patterns, both of those groups will not be successful without very targeted and differentiated lessons.

Areas to Target for Each Group

Mr. Hartline now has three groups of children—children who did well on the oral reading fluency screening (group 3), children who did poorly on the screening, but knew their consonant letter sounds on the phonics inventory (group 2), and children who did poorly on the screening and even on the consonant portion of the letter-sound inventory (group 1). For group 1, his neediest students, Mr. Hartline decides to differentiate in two areas—phonemic awareness and word recognition. For the other two groups, he will concentrate on word recognition and fluency.

Differentiation Strategies in Those Areas

Figure 9.3 provides the strategies and overall focus for Mr. Hartline's whole-group instruction, and Figure 9.4 presents the differentiation strategies he has selected. (If you want to review the instructional strategies, please return to Chapters 3, 4, and 5.) For group 1, the neediest students, he will be especially targeted in his planning. He is sure that the strategies that he has chosen will work well together. He will begin each lesson with oral segmenting and blending exercises to develop phonemic awareness, then provide a brief review of letter names and sounds that

Goal	Materials	Daily activities
• Application of alphabetic principle • Development of word recognition strategies • Development of automatic word recognition skills • Development of oral vocabulary • Development of comprehension strategies	• Core program alphabet manipulatives • Core program big books • Anthology selections • Decodable books • Trade books	• Blending and segmenting • Work with letter patterns • High-frequency-word reading and spelling • Choral and partner reading • Interactive read-alouds with modeling • Explicit vocabulary instruction

FIGURE 9.3. A big-picture plan for first-grade whole-group instruction.

Group 1	Group 2	Group 3
• Phonemic awareness and phonics • Teaching oral segmenting and blending • Teaching letter names and sounds • Say-it-and-move-it • Teaching letter patterns • Teaching high-frequency words	• Word recognition and fluency • Teaching letter patterns • Teaching high-frequency words • Choral partner reading	• Word recognition and fluency • Teaching letter patterns • Teaching high-frequency words • Choral partner reading
Independent extension	Independent extension	Independent extension
Children will practice their letter patterns from small-group instruction with a partner; children will write words with their patterns.	Children will reread their stories from small-group instruction with a partner; children will write a sentence about their fluency story.	Children will use a story map or graphic organizer to write in order to demonstrate comprehension of a story they have heard read aloud.
Small-group center	Small-group center	Small-group center
Children will choose among three small-group centers each day (word work, fluency, listening comprehension), but they must work in each center at least once a week.	Children will choose among three small-group centers each day (word work, fluency, listening comprehension), but they must work in each center at least once a week.	Children will choose among three small-group centers each day (word work, fluency, listening comprehension), but they must work in each center at least once a week.

FIGURE 9.4. A big-picture plan for first-grade small-group differentiated instruction.

are needed in the words that he is teaching in the say-it-and-move-it activity. For say-it-and-move-it, he will use markers the first week, and then, hopefully, move to using letters. Finally, in his work on letter patterns, his goal will be to teach the children short *i* patterns, as most of the children scored well on the short *a* patterns on the phonics inventory, and there are many examples of short *i* patterns in the lessons that he has reviewed in the core. For high-frequency-word instruction, he will reteach the words that these children did not master from the inventory, introducing three new ones each day and also reviewing the words previously taught.

Group 2, the children with adequate letter-sound knowledge, need not work with phonemic awareness during small-group time. Rather, they will focus on both short *i* and short *o*, comparing and contrasting many words containing those two short vowels. These children also have some high-frequency-word work to do, but it will be targeted to those words that any of the children in that group missed on the inventory—there is no need to reteach the entire scope and sequence. Mr. Hartline will also work with fluency for this group, using the decodable texts provided in the program in choral partner reading; using these texts in a review format will provide these students a chance to review previously taught material and build automaticity in word recognition.

The third group, Mr. Hartline's strongest readers, are not yet confident enough to forgo word recognition instruction. Mr. Hartline will reteach the letter patterns and high-frequency words that are targeted in the daily lessons and also use the anthology selections in a choral partner reading format. At least for the first 3 weeks of instruction, Mr. Hartline anticipates that this group will need less of his time. As he works with the class and learns more about the students, he will be able to reteach, preteach, or enrich lessons for this group.

STEP 3: PLAN FOR 3 WEEKS OF INSTRUCTION

Mr. Hartline realizes that the key to his small-group, differentiated instruction is making an integrated plan for group 1. Figure 9.5 is his first attempt. He begins by choosing the words to teach from the high-frequency words in the previous unit that were missed by at least one student in the group. Next, he chooses the letter patterns for the week, and then works backwards, choosing words for say-it-and-

	Week 1	Week 2	Week 3
Oral segmenting and blending	*sit, sat, set* *pin, pan, pen* *top, tap, tip* *pup, pet, sun*	*sun, fun, run* *mop, map, mat* *tin, tan, tan* *hot, hit, hat*	*pick, pack, puck* *tan, ten, tin* *man, mat, map* *sob, job, rob*
Letter names and sounds	*I, N, P, T* *R, S, B, O* *A, D, H, L*	*G, L, M, O* *P, R, A, C* *W, B, I, R*	*J, I, D, A* *K, R, P, E*
Say-it-and-move-it	*pin, tin, fin* *sit, pit, bit* *sip, rip, hip*	*pot, hot, cot* *hop, pop, mop* *rock, sock, lock*	*sip, rip, hip* *top, hop, pop* *sob, job, rob* *sick, pick, lick*
Letter patterns	*-it, -in, -ip*	*-ot, -op, -ock*	*-ip, -op, -ob, -ick*
High-frequency words	*been, very, could,* *live, over*	*look, saw, some,* *once, again*	*give, use, please,* *once, goes*

FIGURE 9.5. A 3-week plan for struggling first graders, group 1.

move-it and for oral segmenting and blending practice that will help the students to practice with the sounds needed to read and spell those words. He thinks in terms of three sets of words or tasks for each strategy, and he knows that he will not be able to teach any of them to mastery in just 1 day. His overall chart is useful, though, because during instruction he can simply cross out those words or tasks that are too easy for the children, thereby honing in on tasks that will have maximum benefit—those tasks that are too difficult for the children to accomplish on their own, but accessible with his modeling and support during the small-group time. Once he has this chart completed for group 1, the same planning sequence is easier to accomplish for groups 2 and 3; this time, though, he starts by looking at the decodable texts that he will use for choral partner reading and plans backwards from there.

STEP 4: PLAN FOR REFLECTION

Mr. Hartline knows that his differentiation plan will not ensure immediate success and that he may have to modify his pacing as he proceeds through the week. He has, however, an organized system for thinking about the needs of the children in his three groups, and he has chosen a flexible set of instructional strategies that he can use for many, many 3-week cycles, changing and gradually increasing the difficulty of the content for each group. He will continue to plan in this way while he is learning more about his students; he will monitor achievement on the tasks that he is choosing during small-group, differentiated instruction and make adjustments as his students acquire new skills and strategies.

CHAPTER 10

A Second-Grade Differentiation Plan

Mrs. Scott has taught first grade for many years, but she is now faced with new data and new pressures—but not a new group of children. She is looping to second grade with her first-grade children from last year. She has traditionally relied on whole-group instruction in a basal reading program, and she has used the program's theme tests to gauge success. By that standard, most of her children have been successful. However, many of last year's third-grade children did not earn proficient scores on the state-mandated third-grade criterion-referenced test, even though many of them appeared to be on target when they were in her first-grade classroom. Given this fact, the school is struggling to meet adequate yearly progress goals, and, if achievement this year is not improved, the school will be sanctioned with a needs-improvement rating. Mrs. Scott herself has been questioning her success as a teacher. In recent years, she has noticed a decline in the quality of discussions during class and in the quality of writing that students are able to produce, not only in terms of mechanics and spelling but content and structure as well.

Mrs. Scott's district has responded to the problematic achievement trends by instituting a new assessment procedure in second grade. They have begun a quarterly benchmarking process. At the start of each marking period, she must assess the entire class with a preselected passage. She is to use the data from her assessments to make instructional groups within her literacy block. Mrs. Scott has always established an orderly classroom, but she is worried about managing the small-group transitions and also about the additional planning that will be involved.

In addition to the new assessment procedure, the district has used its professional development budget in a different way. Beginning this year, Mrs. Scott's building has a literacy coach. Miss Passerell, an experienced classroom teacher and Title I reading specialist, is charged with providing support to the classroom teachers to implement differentiated instruction. Her job is to help teachers interpret assessment data, create classroom schedules, co-plan, model lessons, and observe and give feedback. Mrs. Scott is somewhat skeptical about this idea, but she knows that she may really need help.

STEP 1: GATHER RESOURCES

Mrs. Scott is concerned about the new district plan, but she is even more concerned about meeting the needs of her children. She knows that she will be overwhelmed with the changes unless she starts with a clear idea of what she will use to plan for whole-group and small-group instruction. Miss Passerell helps her.

Curriculum Resources

Mrs. Scott and Miss Passerell review the basal program together to see which portions can be used in small-group instruction, especially for her struggling readers. Figure 10.1 is one of the charts they made to summarize the content of each theme. Mrs. Scott is disappointed. She knows that her children will likely struggle with the lessons, as the decoding demands of the new program are out of sync with the end-of-year skills that she saw at the end of first grade. She is also concerned with the sheer number of activities to be accomplished each day; the transition to the second-grade curriculum will be difficult for many of her students, and also for her.

Mrs. Scott has a classroom library of sets of leveled trade books in addition to her basal program. These books come from the same series as the district benchmark books. However, Mrs. Scott knows that if she simply uses the basal for whole group and the leveled texts for small-group work, she will have to greatly increase the time she spends in literacy activities. She will also likely not really be meeting the needs of all of her students—she knows that leveled books can be used for fluency work, but she also knows that they are unlikely to be helpful with decoding problems.

Assessment Resources

Because Mrs. Scott is interested in the quality of student writing, Miss Passerell advises her to use a spelling inventory in addition to the mandated fluency benchmarking scores. She also encourages Mrs. Scott to use the assessments she has from

Decoding/spelling/ alphabet	Meaning vocabulary	Comprehension skills/strategies
Silent letters (*chalk, thought, gnat, lamb, high, knot, write, sight, crumb, know, wrong, walk, sign*) /er/ (*mother, brother, other, smaller, supper*) short *e* (*head, leather, bread*) long *e* (*tiny, every, happy, penny, many, worry, key, money, donkey, valley, turkey, monkey*)	*decided* *important* *planet* *float* *library* *proud* *climbed* *drifted* *message* *couple* *half* *notice* *arrive* *finish* *rush* *early* *record* *success* *earth* *lonely* *mountain* *forget* *memory* *wonderful* *collect* *join* *pocket* *honor* *order* *worth*	Fantasy/reality Cause and effect Context clues Main idea Make inferences Summarize Analyze characters Recognize setting Use a dictionary Read an encyclopedia Use a telephone directory Choose a reference source

FIGURE 10.1. Second-grade basal scope-and-sequence summary.

her experience in first grade—a high-frequency-word reading inventory and a phonemic awareness battery. Her initial assessment plan is presented in Figure 10.2.

STEP 2: CONSIDER YOUR CHILDREN'S NEEDS

The first benchmark passage looks difficult. She was directed to use an overall accuracy score (percentage of words read correctly) to group children. As Mrs. Scott begins to assess her children, she notices a trend. Many of the students do score at the district-recommended benchmark of at least 95% accuracy on the passage, but

Tool	Purpose
District Benchmark passage 1	Screening
Spelling inventory	Diagnostic measure for children who score below the benchmark
High-frequency word inventory	Diagnostic measure for children who score below the benchmark
Phonemic awareness battery	Diagnostic measure for children who score below the benchmark
District Benchmark passage 2	Progress monitor and new screening

FIGURE 10.2. Assessment plan for Mrs. Scott's second-grade class.

there is great variation in their reading rate. In fact, Mrs. Scott is concerned that students with the same accuracy score will not work together efficiently. With Miss Passerell's help, she begins to track reading rate as well as accuracy. She also notices that overall reading fluency, in terms of accuracy, rate, and prosody, is disappointing. In fact, the initial scores on the benchmarking passage (an early second-grade trade book) hover around 40 words per minute—weak even in first-grade materials.

Mrs. Scott decides to investigate further, with her informal diagnostic measures, all students whose scores on the benchmark were below 95% accuracy or below 40 words per minute. Spelling scores reveal vast differences in understanding of sound–symbol relationships; a small group of students score well (so she assumes that they simply need reading practice) while many others can represent consonant sounds, consonant blends, and digraphs, but are inconsistent with their short vowels. For those students, she also uses the phonemic awareness inventory, but she quickly sees that they score well; the problem lies with phonics knowledge rather than phonemic awareness.

Instructional Groups Based on the Data

Mrs. Scott and Miss Passerell quickly see that there are four groups represented in her data, so the first thing that she considers is her overall instructional diet. She will have to accelerate her whole-group time so that she will be able to spend adequate time with each of the four groups, and she knows that she will have to provide extensive support for fluency. Miss Passerell introduces the concept of fluency-oriented reading instruction. She helps Mrs. Scott to simplify the basal plan (but still use the weekly grade-level anthology story). She will begin the week by reading the story aloud to the children, teaching them meanings of unfamiliar words, and engaging them in structured discussion of the meanings of words. Dur-

Goal	Materials	Daily activities
• Fluency development	• Basal anthology stories • Leveled texts	• Fluency-oriented reading instruction: choral reading, echo reading, partner reading of grade-level text • Partner reading of leveled text
• Vocabulary development	• Basal anthology stories • Children's literature	• Vocabulary discussions
• Comprehension strategies	• Basal anthology stories • Children's literature	• Before-, during-, and after-reading discussions • Direct explanation

FIGURE 10.3. A big-picture plan for second-grade whole-group instruction.

ing the rest of the week, she will gradually decrease her support as she has the children reread the story in echo readings, choral readings, and partner readings. See Figure 10.3 for her overall plan.

Fluency-oriented reading instruction (see Chapter 5 for a review) will provide all of the children access to the grade-level curriculum and also facilitate her small-group, differentiated instruction. The first group, the children about whom she is most concerned, scored poorly on all tasks except those addressed by the phonemic awareness inventory. The second group scored slightly better on the phonics inventory, but these children still lag well behind grade-level achievement in phonics knowledge and in automaticity with high-frequency words—at least as she considers the difficulty in light of the scope and sequence she has reviewed. The third group scored well on the phonics inventory, and had over 90% accuracy on the benchmark fluency passage, but they read in a word-by-word fashion with very slow reading rate. And finally, the fourth group (by far the smallest) was successful on the fluency benchmark. See Figure 10.4 for her overall needs-based plan.

Areas to Target for Each Group

Based on their scores so far, Mrs. Scott knows that her first and second groups both need to work on word recognition and automaticity—but not on the same content. Her third group needs to work on fluency, and she can also use some of her instructional time for comprehension with them. Students with the strongest skills, group 4, can work on vocabulary and comprehension. They will receive

Group 1	Group 2	Group 3	Group 4
• Word recognition and fluency • Teaching sounding and blending • Teaching high-frequency words • Choral partner reading	• Word recognition and fluency • Teaching letter patterns • Teaching high-frequency words • Choral partner reading	• Fluency and comprehension • Repeated reading • Question-and-answer relationships	• Fluency and comprehension • Repeated reading • Story mapping
Independent extension	Independent extension	Independent extension	Independent extension
Partner activities with vowel families and then with decodable texts	Partner reading with decodable and then leveled texts	Partner reading with leveled texts	Partner reading and summary generation

FIGURE 10.4. A big-picture plan for second-grade differentiated needs-based instruction.

grade-level fluency work as part of FORI every day, so she does not need to attend to it during small-group time.

Differentiation Strategies in Those Areas

Miss Passerell must help Mrs. Scott design a plan that helps her *and* the students to become accustomed to working in small groups. Mrs. Scott knows that teachers of younger children rely on centers, but she is uncomfortable with that concept. Miss Passerell begins by thinking about what children can do during work with other small groups. She decides that partner reading with another member of the group will be easy for Mrs. Scott to manage and it will increase the total number of words each child reads each day manyfold. It will help Mrs. Scott manage materials and provide some differentiated oral reading practice to complement the grade-level practice that will come as part of her FORI plan.

Miss Passerell also decides that Mrs. Scott will have an extension activity derived from each day's small-group instruction, an activity that focuses additional attention on the area that she is targeting. For groups 1 and 2, working on word recognition, she will provide first-grade texts and ask the children to read to find words with the same patterns as the ones they are studying. They can write these words in their marble pads as additional examples and practice with the letter sounds and patterns they are learning.

STEP 3: PLAN FOR 3 WEEKS OF INSTRUCTION

Planning a scope and sequence for that instruction is the challenging part of Mrs. Scott's differentiation plan, but Miss Passerell helps her. For her group with the largest needs, she feels confident that she needs to review almost all of the phonics content from the previous year's instruction. Either her strategies or her pacing or both were not consistent with the needs of these children to build and apply firm knowledge of letter–sound relationships. She decides that she will reteach the first-grade phonics curriculum in total, beginning with the 4th week of instruction (the time in the program that constitutes new information after an initial review of the kindergarten curriculum). She sees that she will need only a manual to prepare this instruction, as she will not use workbooks or readers and will be able to make word cards for modeling and practice. She plans to teach each week's content in 2 days, and to review on the 5th day. At that accelerated rate, she should be able to work through all of the first-grade phonics content in about 12 weeks, and she can change her pacing as students build skills or struggle with the concepts. For high-frequency words, she will rely on the data from her inventory and also include new words from the second-grade scope and sequence.

For group 2, reteaching of first-grade concepts would not be appropriate; their phonics inventory data suggest that they know their consonants and digraphs, have some trouble with the short vowels, and even more trouble with r-controlled and long vowels. She plans to reteach all of the most frequent short-vowel families during the course of the 3-week segment of instruction. She targets three sets of three patterns for each week, reserving 2 days for reviewing and combining the patterns. Once she has chosen her patterns, it is very simple to generate lists of words for each; she does this by taking an alphabet strip and adding every consonant to each of the patterns; if that combination constitutes a real word, she writes it on a word card and files it in a recipe box.

Finding ways for children to practice the patterns in some form of connected text is more difficult to plan. Miss Passerell gives her a book of poems constructed to highlight vowel patterns (Rasinski & Zimmerman, 2001). This text provides simple poems that she can duplicate for student use in repeated readings. They make file folders for each pattern, including the word cards and the practice poems, so that management of materials during instruction will be smooth.

Once Mrs. Scott has worked with Miss Passerell to plan for groups 1 and 2, she feels more confident that she will be able to differentiate instruction. She sees, too, that if she commits to using the same instructional strategies over and over while changing the content, she will not have to teach the children how to participate in too many different strategies. She also sees that her instructional planning time is spent in a very meaningful way—she is thinking about what the students need to learn about print and text rather than trying to create new instructional strategies.

For group 3, the group with adequate word recognition and decoding skills but weak reading rate, Mrs. Scott decides to use the first-grade anthology stories beginning midway through the year. She can easily borrow five copies of the anthology from the book room, and she does not need to use the teacher's manual. She gathers a timer and some recording sheets to chart student progress. In addition, she copies story maps and a summary sheet that will also be used in her whole-group work. For this group, the challenge will be where to start. She estimates that the mid-first-grade texts will provide adequate challenge without frustration, but she cannot be sure. During the first days of small-group instruction, she will experiment until she finds a passage that seems right for the group, and then she will move to the next passage as soon as the children meet the 100-word-per-minute criterion.

The last group, those whose current achievement is at least at grade level, is simple to prepare for. For that group, she will reteach the Tier 2 words from her read-aloud, this time with the goal of reading and spelling in addition to meaning. She will also use the story maps and the summary sheet, alternating attention between the anthology story used in FORI and the day's read-aloud. Given small-group time with this group, Mrs. Scott will have an opportunity to challenge them through comprehension and writing tasks that stretch their skills. See Figure 10.5 for an overview of her 3-week plan.

STEP 4: PLAN FOR REFLECTION

Mrs. Scott's fears about the progress of her children are somewhat allayed after she develops a plan of action. She knows it will not be an easy plan to implement because her past experience has been with whole-group instruction. However, she

	Week 1	**Week 2**	**Week 3**
Phonics sounding and blending	*M, P, T, R* *a-n, a-p, a-t* *F, C, R, L* *o-t, o-p, o-c-k*	*B, H, C, S* *i-t, i-n, i-p* *D, G, N, V* *u-n, u-p, u-t*	*SH, CH* *e-n, e-d, e-t* *TH* Short *a*, short *o*
High-frequency words	*like, me, I, the, am,* *went, to, my*	*are, we, is, mouse,* *she, man, once*	*with, have, give,* *when, look, said*
Fluency	*an, at, ock,* and *ot* poems	*in, ip, up* and *un* poems	Short-vowel poems
Word hunt	Basal decodable story	Basal decodable story	Basal decodable story

FIGURE 10.5. A 3-week plan for struggling second graders, group 1.

has come to question the wisdom of that approach and knows that for the good of her children she must do a better job of addressing their specific needs. Her familiarity with the first-grade materials will make her use of those materials fairly easy, but she knows she will be facing a substantial challenge in managing small-groups. It is a challenge she is ready for.

Miss Passerell asks Mrs. Scott what she would like in terms of support. Mrs. Scott asks that she not observe or help during the first week's instruction; Mrs. Scott wants to try to get the management in place on her own. She asks, however, that they meet after school at the end of the first week, and consider a modeling or observation visit during week 2. Miss Passerell and Mrs. Scott have gotten off to a good start, and Mrs. Scott feels ready to give differentiation a try.

CHAPTER 11

A Third-Grade Differentiation Plan

Mrs. Beale has taught third grade for many years, and she is always ready for a new curricular challenge. This year, the district has begun an experiment with clustered grouping—and Mrs. Beale is the logical choice given her experience. Her homeroom will have both the five children who qualify for gifted and talented services and the four third graders who qualify for special education resource services in reading; they are included during the full 2-hour language arts block, and Mrs. Hayes, a special educator, partners with her for 45 minutes. The 14 other children represent a range of skills.

Mrs. Beale has learned that third graders benefit from both structure and personal responsibility. She teaches them to work in many different groupings and to take care of one another. Her classroom has always had a good sense of identity as a group, mostly because Mrs. Beale takes the time to teach procedures for working together. These priorities will serve her well as she plans for the clustered groups.

STEP 1: GATHER RESOURCES

Collaboration with Mrs. Hayes provides a chance for Mrs. Beale to streamline her small-group plan. She has always been able to meet daily with small groups, but not with every group every day. Given the planned diversity in her class this year, Mrs. Beale wants to consider a plan that brings each group to her each day. She also wants to be sure that Mrs. Hayes's work with her students represents additional time and instruction for them.

Curriculum Resources

Mrs. Beale's core program for third grade is not very explicit. There are decoding lessons, but they are not especially geared to the real challenge of third-grade decoding: multisyllabic words. Figure 11.1 contains Mrs. Beale's notes for the first theme. She will capitalize on the fact that there are many instances for comparing and contrasting vowel patterns. Mrs. Beale also has a set of self-paced reading comprehension exercises that she can use for fluency and comprehension practice. She has a large classroom library of information trade books matched to the content of her state social studies and science curricula. She also has a smaller library of narrative trade books, mostly series books that she has found that third graders

Decoding/spelling/ alphabet	Meaning vocabulary	Comprehension skills/strategies
Long a, -aime, -ain, -ay	imaginary	Cause and effect
Short a, -ack, -ang	miserable	Comparison and contrast
/a/ and /e/	shallow	Make judgments and decisions
/ch/	stump	Predictions
consonant	adobe	Character
/sh/	thatched	Plot
/i/ and /e/	delighted	Mood
-est	directly	Techniques of persuasion
/e/ and long e, spelled ea	route	Summarize
	strength	Author's purpose and point of view
	disguised	Evaluate fact and non-fact
	furious	Form generalizations
	difficult	Main idea and supporting details
	discovered	Important and unimportant information
	expects	
	magnified	
	underneath	
	beliefs	
	temperature	
	fable	
	equipment	
	explorer	
	pollution	
	precious	
	surface	
	depths	
	endangered	
	pressure	

FIGURE 11.1. Third-grade scope-and-sequence summary.

enjoy. She uses these books in lieu of worksheets for morning work; all students begin the day with wide reading and read until the morning announcement. This procedure ensures a quiet morning routine and also squeezes as many as 20 minutes of additional reading time into the instructional day. By carefully establishing routines at the beginning of the school year, she ensures that children enter the classroom with a clear idea of what they are to do.

The core anthology is structured so that one story is read each week, with a variety of activities to develop vocabulary knowledge and comprehension during guided readings and rereadings. Her experience with her core reading program tells her that she should use the anthology story for whole-group modeling, but that the guided reading portion of that story should be conducted in the small-group setting. Whole-group guided reading does not provide her children with enough interaction with the text.

Assessment Resources

Mrs. Beale's district uses a comprehensive screening battery at the beginning and middle of each year. That screening includes a grade-level word recognition test, a spelling test, an oral reading fluency test, and a passage followed by comprehension questions. Data are used to identify children who are at risk, and potentially to select them for additional instruction with the Title I reading specialist. For third grade, however, no Title I services are available. Mrs. Beale uses the data to form her small groups and she also conducts an after-school book club for those students who are below grade level.

Mrs. Beale is famous for her November challenge. At that time, she gives a 200-word spelling test of high-frequency words, and she has always had 100% success. She accomplishes this by really targeting these words; at the beginning of the year, she gives a pretest to all of the students. They score their own spellings, and make two sets of flash cards for the ones that they don't know. Each student's cards are hole-punched and stored on a metal ring, hung on a hook in the classroom; the other set is kept in the student's book bag for work at home. Those students whose initial scores are perfect get a ring of content-area words from the state curriculum.

Fluency has been a concern at the school level, and the principal has analyzed data across classrooms. Given the current curriculum, 75% of the children make adequate progress in word recognition, but only 50% achieve fluency benchmarks over time. Each teacher has a set of graded fluency passages that can be used both for assessment and for repeated readings; the passages are relatively short and formatted for collection of data on children's reading rate and accuracy.

This year, Mrs. Beale also has the comprehensive assessments of her children qualifying for special education. This is the first time that she has been able to look across such tests for common elements among the students. At first she sees that there are weaknesses in every part of the reading puzzle, but then she sees that all of her special education children struggle specifically in the area of word recognition. Two of them also have fairly weak oral language comprehension, but the other three have normal language comprehension. Taken together, then, Mrs. Beale's beginning-of-the-year assessment plan is reproduced in Figure 11.2.

Mrs. Beale confers with Mrs. Hayes about curriculum resources that she can bring to the classroom; Mrs. Hayes has a comprehensive decoding intervention program. She can use the placement test from that program to know where to start her instruction. The program targets synthetic decoding, then vowel patterns, and finally decoding-by-analogy strategies. Based on the special education testing, it seems logical that these students will be working with short vowel patterns.

STEP 2: CONSIDER YOUR CHILDREN'S NEEDS

Mrs. Beale wants to target her instruction so that she can maximize children's instruction and practice time in actual reading and writing and focus most of her own attention on scaffolding during reading. She will target both word recognition and comprehension. She decides that she will begin each day with an information-book read-aloud. She knows that third graders love to learn about the world, and this strategy helps her to develop the vocabulary and concept knowledge that children need for success in third grade. During that time, she will take the opportunity to model comprehension strategies that have been taught previously and to use semantic feature analysis charts to compare and contrast concepts.

She also knows that third graders typically still need more instruction in decoding, and she wants to be sure that she provides it in a strategic way. She decides that, in general, she will use the core decoding lesson each day to model strategies for decoding the target words in the core and also any words from her high-frequency list that have the same patterns.

Tool	Purpose
District beginning-of-year battery	Screening
High-frequency-word test	Screening
Comprehensive achievement battery	Diagnostic measure for special-education students
Fluency passages	Progress monitoring

FIGURE 11.2. Assessment plan for Mrs. Beale's third-grade class.

Finally, she sees the need to teach directly the comprehension strategy selected for each anthology story. There is a script for doing so in the core, and she plans to use it to introduce the anthology story each day. After that introduction, though, she will use paired reading (rather than whole-group guided reading) to maximize engagement. For the special education students with decoding problems, she will partner one of her strongest readers and ask the stronger reader to read aloud and the weaker reader to track the print. As soon as that procedure is completed she can begin to meet with her groups. An overview of Mrs. Beale's plan for whole-group instruction appears in Figure 11.3.

Instructional Groups Based on the Data

Mrs. Beale knows that she will have a decoding group, and that this group will meet with Mrs. Hayes for 45 minutes. She imagines that this group will include the special education students and perhaps one or two other readers whose screening data indicate decoding problems. That will mean that there are 15–17 other children to meet with during that time; Mrs. Beale decides that she will divide them into three groups based on their oral reading fluency and meet with them for 15 minutes each. (One of these groups consists of the highest-achieving children—potentially all of the gifted children, but not necessarily—and the other two are average.) At the end of Mrs. Hayes's lesson, she will meet Mrs. Hayes's group for 15 minutes. Small-group time, then, will comprise 60 minutes in all. The schedule appears in Figure 11.4.

Areas to Target for Each Group

Mrs. Beale will work on word recognition, vocabulary, and fluency with her two middle groups. In addition, group 1 will work on decoding with Mrs. Hayes and then fluency with Mrs. Beale. Group 4 will work on vocabulary and fluency. Mrs. Beale is very concerned that the rest of the instructional time (45 minutes in all) is well structured and she provides each student with maximum opportunities for challenging work.

Goal	Materials	Daily activities
• Vocabulary and concept knowledge • Decoding by analogy • Fluency and comprehension	• Information trade books • Core decoding lesson and high-frequency words • Core anthology stories	• Interactive read-aloud • Direct explanation • Paired reading

FIGURE 11.3. A big-picture plan for third-grade whole-group instruction.

Teacher	15 minutes	15 minutes	15 minutes	15 minutes
Beale	Average-achieving children (group 2)	Average-achieving children (group 3)	Highest-achieving children (group 4)	Mrs. Hayes's group (group 1)
Hayes	Special-education children plus other struggling readers (group 1)			Mrs. Hayes moves to another classroom

FIGURE 11.4. Small-group schedule for Mrs. Beale and Mrs. Hayes.

Differentiation Strategies in Those Areas

Mrs. Beale is confident that the same instructional strategies will work with groups 2 and 3. For them, she will begin by modeling decoding by analogy with the basal words and with words on her word wall. She will then try to model decoding of two multisyllabic words each day. For vocabulary, she will use the Tier 2 word strategy, reviewing the words she has introduced in whole group and allowing each student the chance to produce a new sentence context for the words. For fluency, she will use choral partner reading if the text is very difficult for the group, or paired rereading if it is relatively easy.

For group 4, for whom decoding is not an issue at all, she will begin with vocabulary, again reviewing the Tier 2 words. This time, though, instead of orally producing a new context, she will ask the children to write their new sentence down, encouraging them to expand their sentences to encompass more precise meanings and to include more than a single new word in the same sentence. For fluency, because it is substituting for the whole-group guided reading, she will have the children read orally (but not chorally) while she listens to individuals. She imagines that one reading of the day's text will be enough.

For group 1, which has begun the small-group rotation working with Mrs. Hayes on decoding, Mrs. Beale wants to ensure maximum exposure to the ideas and vocabulary of the anthology selection. She knows, though, that it is likely to be much too hard. She will use echo reading to support the students, moving to choral reading if possible. She will end by discussing the story's meaning.

Rather than establish centers or assign different work to each group, Mrs. Beale decides to structure a work plan for the entire week. She will assign partners at the beginning of each week; that way, some weeks she can partner two readers matched on skills and during other weeks she can partner two children with different skills. Those partners will be responsible for working together during partner time to produce high-quality work in a particular order, which they will document in a work chart. This chart is reproduced in Figure 11.5. She will meet with the

Step 1: Paired rereading of weekly story		
• We read the text aloud ___ times.	• We stopped because we could read it quickly and easily.	• We stopped because we had practiced five times.

Step 2: High-frequency-word practice		
• We chose 10 of our words to practice.	• We read them to one another until they were easy.	• We took a spelling test and got ___ correct.

Step 3: Summary of daily text		
• We discussed the main idea in today's reading.	• We used the summary sheet to plan a summary.	• We edited our summary until it was our best work.

Step 4: Concept of definition map		
• We selected a map for _____.	• We filled in the map to review the meaning.	• We used the map to write a fantastic sentence.

Step 5: Feature analysis		
• We selected a feature analysis for _____.	• We talked about similarities and differences.	• We used the FA to write a fantastic paragraph about one idea.

Step 6: Summary of read-aloud		
• We used a summary checklist.	• We planned our summary together.	• We wrote a fantastic summary.

Step 7: Independent comprehension activity		
• We chose a comprehension lesson.	• We did it together.	• We checked our work and got ___ correct.

Step 8: New paired reading		
• We chose a book because _____.	• We read a few pages to see if it was a good fit.	• We read it and learned that _____.

FIGURE 11.5. Chart for differentiated partner work for third grade.

pairs on Fridays before dismissal to help them to produce a self-evaluation of their use of time during the week; that evaluation will go home to their families in their Friday folder, along with selections from the week's partner work. An overview of Mrs. Beale's plan for needs-based group instruction appears in Figure 11.6.

STEP 3: PLAN FOR 3 WEEKS OF INSTRUCTION

Mrs. Beale's planning includes two basic procedures. First, she must use the basal decoding lesson to plan her decoding-by-analogy procedure. Then, she must choose information texts to read aloud and prepare concept of definition and semantic feature analysis charts. The fluency passages she will use (at least for the beginning of the year) are the basal anthology selections; she will alter her scaffolding and support rather than altering the text that the students read.

For the first theme, the basal targets long- and short-*a* patterns and long- and short-*e* patterns. From her high-frequency list, she chooses *she, here, hear, many,* and *field,* and she elects to model decoding words with long-*e* sounds. She chooses *bacon, train, play, eight,* and *fake* to model decoding words with long *a* sounds. For each of those words, she makes a list of words to decode by analogy, focusing on the vowel patterns. That list is reproduced in Figure 11.7. She sees quickly that these words will provide opportunities for vocabulary lessons as well.

To start her read-aloud/vocabulary lessons, she collects social studies trade books about geography. She can quickly prepare a semantic feature analysis chart comparing cities, suburbs, and rural regions. She can also prepare concept of definition maps for each of these terms singly, and also for the concepts of climate, weather, culture, economy, and currency. She makes an additional semantic fea-

Group 1	Group 2	Group 3	Group 4
• Decoding • Fluency • Teaching letter patterns • Echo reading	• Word recognition • Vocabulary • Fluency • Decoding by analogy • Choral partner reading	• Word recognition • Vocabulary • Fluency • Decoding by analogy • Rereading	• Vocabulary • Fluency • Tier 2 words • Rereading
	Partner time	Partner time	Partner time
Paired rereading of daily text; high-frequency-word practice; summary of daily text; concept of definition map; semantic feature analysis; summary of read-aloud; independent comprehension activities; new paired reading from classroom library			

FIGURE 11.6. A big-picture plan for third-grade differentiated needs-based instruction.

she	hear	here	many	field
being	beaver	delete	angry	achieve
fever	appeal	complete	beauty	relieve
female	creature	supreme	county	diesel
legal	eager	precede	gravy	belief
veto	ideal	trapeze	guilty	retrieve
decent	reason	extreme	tidy	yield
bacon	**train**	**play**	**eight**	**fake**
basic	sailor	mayor	reign	maze
lazy	refrain	crayon	veil	debate
shaky	remain	decay	vein	bracelet
patient	trainer	layer	weight	persuade
fable	dainty	today	freight	safety
agent	afraid	betray	neighbor	skateboard

FIGURE 11.7. Words to decode by analogy.

ture analysis chart for the economics standards targeting consumers and produc-
ers.

STEP 4: PLAN FOR REFLECTION

Mrs. Beale knows that her plan is just a plan, and that she will have to adjust as she gets to know the skills and strategies of her class more deeply. She knows, too, that she can regroup quickly if she has made errors, and that the weekly pairs will give her additional chances to match children to one another and to challenging tasks and content. She looks forward to a differentiation plan that relies both on the formal data from her screening and diagnostic measures and on the informal data that she will get from her own interactions with the children during instruction. Differentiation for small groups in third grade demands a flexible stance toward children and a deep concern with developing knowledge and skills. Mrs. Beale brings those characteristics into her classroom every day.

Glossary of Reading Terms

accuracy: the successful pronunciation of words encountered in print; sometimes contrasted with speed.

assessment-driven instruction: instruction that is planned on the basis of screening and diagnostic testing designed to reveal a child's specific needs; such assessments are subsequently repeated and modified as instruction proceeds.

automaticity: the point at which word identification is so rapid it requires no conscious attention.

basal reader: a textbook designed to improve reading ability; contains selections at roughly the same level of readability (see **core instructional materials**).

basal reading series: an organized series of materials, including leveled readers, workbooks, etc.; the rationale is that children should be placed in the series at an appropriate point and then allowed to move through the remaining levels (see **core instructional materials**).

big book: an oversized book used to model the reading process, to teach conventions of print, and to conduct decoding instruction on a teachable-moment basis.

blend: *See* **consonant blend.**

blending: pronouncing a word by pronouncing each phoneme in sequence.

clustered grouping: an approach to controlling (without eliminating) the heterogeneity of a classroom by assigning a limited number of "clusters" to a homeroom—for example, a classroom might have several gifted students and several students with LDs in addition to average students; this system of assigning children to rooms is intended to make group formation more manageable than random placement and also to avoid the pitfalls of tracking.

compound word: a word consisting of two or more root words that have not been altered in forming the compound (examples: *farmhand*, *gingerbread*); some linguists consider certain physically divided words, like *high school*, to be compounds, but this is not an important distinction in reading instruction since the white space allows each part to be identified separately; in compound words written as a single word, children must learn to recognize the components.

comprehension: "the process of simultaneously extracting and constructing meaning through interaction and involvement with written language" (RAND Reading Study Group, 2002, p. xiii).

comprehension monitoring: continuously checking one's own understanding during reading; a form of metacognition.

comprehension strategy: any of several techniques employed by proficient readers to ensure adequate comprehension; such strategies include activating prior knowledge, setting specific purposes for reading, predicting, summarizing, visualizing, and employing "fix-up" techniques like rereading.

consolidated alphabetic phase: the fourth and final phase of the decoding stage of reading development; during this phase, children can apply extensive knowledge of the alphabetic principle, including knowledge of spelling patterns, to pronounce most novel words (cf. **prealphabetic phase, partial alphabetic phase, full alphabetic phase**).

consonant blend: two or more consonants appearing together in a word and representing the sound of each individual consonant (examples: *bl* in *blend*, and *nd* in *blend*).

consonant cluster: two or more consonants appearing together in a word.

consonant digraph: two consonants appearing together in a word and representing a sound not associated with either consonant individually (examples: *sh*, *ch*, *th*, *ph*, *ng*).

context clue: any clue about the meaning of a word derived from the surrounding words or pictures.

control group: in experimental and quasiexperimental research, a group of individuals against whom the effects of an educational treatment, technique, or intervention are gauged; control group members usually receive instruction that is considered conventional in nature.

core instructional materials: the main commercial reading program (usually a basal series) used in an elementary school; the core program may be supplemented by additional programs, trade books, etc.

curriculum-based assessment: an approach to assessment that uses children's performance with curricular materials to make judgments about instructional growth and needs (e.g., a basal passage might be used to assess oral reading fluency).

curriculum map: a system that places key objectives and standards in a logical sequence and relates them to instructional activities that are designed to help children attain them; recommended assessments are sometimes included.

decodable book: a book consisting solely of words that are regular in terms of letter–sound relationships; exceptions (e.g., *of*, *who*) are excluded.

decoding: analyzing an unfamiliar word in order to arrive at its pronunciation.

decoding by analogy: determining the pronunciation of a word encountered in print by comparing it with one or more words already familiar to the reader (e.g., to pronounce the nonsense word *zum*, a proficient reader might relate it to the word *gum* rather than attempt to blend the individual phonemes); for multisyllabic words, the process is more complex and may involve two or more known words (e.g., the word *bandiferous* might be likened to *band*, *different*, and *generous*).

diagnostic assessment: a test that is typically administered to identify specific instructional needs after a screening assessment has indicated a general weakness in a given area (e.g., a phonics screening test might be followed by a phonics inventory to identify specific skill deficits).

diphthong: a combination of two vowels in which the sound of the first glides seamlessly into the second (example: oi in *oil*, ou in *our*).

direct explanation: teaching that focuses specifically on a skill or strategy in such a way that it is presented (explained), its use is modeled, and its application by the child is monitored and assisted until it can be applied independently; direct explanation can be contrasted with incidental instruction that is not systematic and the focus of which does not center on the skill or strategy; also called direct instruction or explicit instruction.

direct instruction: *See* direct explanation.

experimental research: any investigation that compares two conditions (e.g., two instructional approaches) by analyzing pre- and postassessments after controlling for potentially contributing factors; for example, an experiment to determine the effectiveness of Technique A might involve two groups of children, one receiving Treatment A and the other Treatment B; because success might be expected to relate to factors other than the instructional method, the children's reading ability, cultural background, gender, and other factors might be accounted for statistically.

explicit instruction: *See* direct explanation.

expository text: a form of nonfiction that is not organized chronologically but is structured instead according to subtopics, arguments, etc.

false negative: a test result indicating that a child possesses a skill or proficiency when in fact there is a deficit.

false positive: a test result indicating that a child lacks a skill or proficiency when in fact it has been attained.

fiction: collectively, any of several prose genres (e.g., novel, short story) representing imaginary events and characters, though real events and characters may be incorporated as well.

fingerpoint reading: a form of oral reading in which the child points to each word as he or she reads it aloud; such pointing can provide information about whether the child is adequately tracking and is recognizing printed word boundaries.

fluency: the developmental stage at which word recognition is quick and phrasing is adultlike; this stage is thought to lie between the stage during which a child learns to decode and the stage at which the child can effectively learn from printed sources;

note that this term is sometimes extended to any set of skills that a child can apply automatically, such as letter naming or phoneme segmentation.

frustration level: the lowest readability level at which comprehension is poor even when instructional support is available; sometimes defined in terms of actual emotional frustration.

full alphabetic phase: the third phase of the decoding stage of reading development; during this phase, children are able to use letter-sound knowledge to blend the phonemes of a printed word in order to approximate its pronunciation, but advanced spelling patterns still present problems (cf. **prealphabetic phase, partial alphabetic phase, consolidated alphabetic phase**).

genre: an established form of writing with agreed-upon conventions (examples: novel, short story, lyric poem, limerick, news story, essay).

grapheme: a letter or letter combination representing a single phoneme (example: *f* and *ph* are graphemes that represent the phoneme /f/).

graphic organizer: a diagram showing how key terms are related (example: timelines, Venn diagrams, tree diagrams, sociograms, labeled pictures); some definitions include charts.

high-frequency word: a word that occurs so often in text that readers must be able to pronounce it automatically in order to achieve fluency; examples include function words, like prepositions, conjunctions, and the like, but also many content words, such colors, animals, days of the week, etc. (cf. **sight word**).

independent level: the highest readability level at which comprehension is good, even when instructional support is unavailable; books at the independent level tend to make good library books and good choices for Sustained Silent Reading (SSR) and Drop Everything and Read (DEAR).

inference: a logical conclusion arrived at on the basis of stated facts and/or facts known to the reader prior to reading; inferences can be certain or merely probable, depending on the available facts; "a statement about the unknown made on the basis of the known" (S. I. Hayakawa).

inflectional ending: any one of a limited set of suffixes that change a word in a minor way, such as number or tense; these endings include *-s, -es, -d, -ed,* and *-ing*.

informal assessments: tests that have few specific requirements as to how they are administered and scored, leaving much to the discretion of the teacher; such tests are never interpreted through the use of norms since the conditions under which they are given can vary considerably.

informal reading inventory (IRI): an assessment instrument consisting primarily of a sequence of passages of known readability; by asking a child to read several of the passages, one can estimate the child's instructional reading level on the basis of word recognition errors and comprehension performance.

instructional level: the highest readability level at which a child can read with good comprehension as long as instructional support is available; textbooks are best when they are at the instructional level.

invented spelling: spelling that reflects a child's knowledge of letter–sound relationships, through the errors it contains; considered by some to be a good way to allow children to explore phonics, though educators debate the proper transition into correct spelling.

leveled texts: short trade books sequenced by difficulty level and used in small-group instruction, usually in the primary grades.

lexicon: (1) all of the words that are meaningful to an individual; (2) that part of semantic memory where such words are stored; (3) all of the words that constitute a language at any given time.

long vowel: a vowel sound associated with the name of the vowel letter (examples: *a* in *lane*, *e* in *lean*, *i* in *line*, *o* in *lone*, *u* in *lute*); note that long *u* imperfectly expresses the letter name of *u*.

mnemonic strategies: a method of teaching and learning that focuses on remembering a word or fact based on an unusual association (e.g., children are sometimes taught that the word *look* contains two "eyes" or that the colors of the visible spectrum can be recalled in order by remembering the name "Roy G. Biv": red, orange, yellow, green, blue, indigo, violet).

modeling: demonstrating how a skill or strategy is properly applied.

morpheme: the smallest unit of meaning in a language; the term applies to words (e.g., *cat*) and to letters (e.g., *-s*) so that *cats* contains two morphemes; a distinction is sometimes made between free morphemes (those, like *cat*, that can stand alone) and bound morphemes (those like *-s* that have meaning only when attached to a free morpheme).

nonfiction: collectively, any of several prose genres (e.g., essay, biography, textbook) presenting factual information and involving actual events and persons; nonfiction may have an expository or narrative organization.

onset: the consonant or consonant cluster that begins a word (cf. **rime**).

onset–rime awareness: the understanding that most syllables can be pronounced by rendering them into two parts: (1) the initial consonant or consonant cluster and (2) the vowel and following consonants.

partial alphabetic phase: the second phase of the decoding stage of reading development; during this phase, children are able to use limited letter-sound knowledge to pronounce written words, but they are usually unsuccessful; for example, *gem* might be read as *gum* (cf. **prealphabetic phase, full alphabetic phase, consolidated alphabetic phase**).

phoneme: the smallest recognizable unit of sound in a language; the word *cat* contains three phonemes, *the* two, *great* four.

phoneme categorization: given a set of one-syllable spoken words all but one of which share a phoneme (e.g., *pig, pack, put, run*), the ability to identify which word in the group does not belong with the others; also known as phoneme identification.

phoneme isolation: given a spoken word, the ability to say one phoneme when provided its location (e.g., "What is the middle sound of *pat*? or "What is the beginning sound of *leap*?").

phonemic awareness: cognizance of the phonemes that make up spoken words; this ability is causally related to learning to read (cf. **phonological awareness**).

phonetically regular word: a printed word whose pronunciation can be determined on the basis of common, frequently occurring orthographic structures; in reality regularity is a matter of degree—for example, everyone would agree that *red* is regular because each letter represents a phoneme, because these letter–sound relationships are familiar, and because the pronunciation of *red* can be approximated by blending these three phonemes; however, the word *of* is generally thought to be irregular, but only because the phonemes /u/ and /v/ are hardly ever associated with the letters *o* and *f*.

phonetic cue reading: word reading that is characterized by some knowledge of letter-sound relationships for real words; this knowledge is not yet sufficient to permit the child to pronounce pseudowords (see **partial alphabetic phase**).

phonics: instruction in reading and spelling that stresses letter–sound relationships.

phonogram: a familiar word element used to form a word family; consists of a vowel or vowel combination followed by a consonant or consonant combination (examples: *-at, -ight, -ain*); same as **rime**.

phonological awareness: cognizance of any of the component speech sounds that make up spoken words; while not directly connected to written language, this ability is a prerequisite for learning phonics; this term includes not only an awareness of phonemes but of larger units as well, like rimes (cf. **phonemic awareness**).

prealphabetic phase: the first phase of the decoding stage of reading development; during this phase, children have almost no letter-sound knowledge and may use the first letter of a word or environmental clues to guess at the pronunciation (cf. **partial alphabetic phase, full alphabetic phase, consolidated alphabetic phase**).

prefix: a letter or letter combination that, when added to the beginning of a word, changes its meaning.

prevention-based instruction: instruction in which predictive assessments are used to establish a degree of risk and proactive steps are taken before the problem becomes hard to manage; such instruction can be contrasted with intervention-based instruction, which follows the identification of a major problem.

progress monitoring assessment: a test that is administered periodically after an intervention has begun in order to determine its impact and whether to modify or discontinue it.

prosody: a component of oral reading fluency that is characterized by appropriate, expressive phrasing and intonation; prosody depends on automatic, accurate word recognition but adds another dimension—think of the difference between an auctioneer and an actor.

***r*-controlled vowel:** a vowel followed by the letter *r*, which causes the vowel to have a sound that is neither long nor short (examples: *a* in *car*, *e* in *her*); sometimes called the "bossy *r*."

rate: speed of reading, typically expressed as either the number of words per minute (wpm) or the number of words correctly read per minute (wcpm).

readability: the estimated difficulty level of a particular selection, generally expressed as a grade level.

readability formula: a method of estimating readability by systematically considering certain factors, such as word length, sentence length, etc.; most formulas provide a way of arriving at a grade-level estimate.

Reading First: a large-scale K–3 federal program through which funded schools apply scientifically based reading instruction, employ literacy coaches, and plan instruction based on periodic screening assessments.

Reading Recovery: a first-grade intervention program designed to accelerate the progress of poor readers before they fall too far behind; originated in New Zealand.

regular word: *See* **phonetically regular word.**

reliable assessment: a test that tends to produce similar results under similar circumstances; factors that increase reliability include the clarity of directions, the structure of test items, and the length of the test; reliability is a prerequisite to validity (cf. **valid assessment**).

rhyme awareness: cognizance that two spoken words share the same ending vowel–consonant combination.

rime: a phonogram; this spelling distinguishes the concept from the poetic device (examples: in the word *cat*, the rime is *at*, in *bite* the rime is *ite*) (cf. **onset**).

root word: a word that has been altered by the addition of one or more affixes.

scope and sequence: a reading skills curriculum organized by the order in which the skills are taught and reinforced; the organizing rationale behind a basal reading series.

screening assessment: a test designed to provide a quick indication of whether a problem exists in a broad area; without more, screening assessments can do little to help with instructional planning (cf. **diagnostic assessment**).

segmenting: the ability to partition a spoken word into constituent sounds, such as phonemes, syllables, or onset and rime.

semantics: the study of how words express and represent meaning.

short vowel: a vowel sound typically heard in consonant–vowel–consonant words (*a* in *pat*, *e* in *pet*, *i* in *pit*, *o* in *pot*, *u* in *pub*).

sight word: any word that can be pronounced immediately, at sight, without conscious analysis; this term is not synonymous with *high-frequency words*, although most high-frequency words eventually become sight words; whether a word is a sight word depends on the individual (cf. **high-frequency word**).

skills: specific proficiencies that are largely independent of a particular context or purpose for reading; skills, like tools, may be more or less relevant to a particular occasion (comprehension skills might include inferring a cause-and-effect relationship or noting an explicitly stated fact) (cf. **strategies**).

sociocultural factors: related social and cultural factors that might influence literacy learning or the application of literacy skills and strategies; for example, instruction based on interaction among students assumes that learning is optimized through social interplay.

strategies: proficiencies that involve the application of skills to achieve a particular goal, depending on the context of and purpose for reading (comprehension strategies might include predicting an outcome or generating self-questions to guide thinking) (cf. **skills**).

suffix: a letter or letter combination that, when added to the end of a word, changes its meaning.

syllable: a unit of spoken language that consists of a vowel sound and, typically, one or more adjacent consonant sounds.

syllable awareness: the understanding that spoken words comprise one or more syllables; this understanding is usually reflected in the ability to segment spoken words into syllables or to identify the original word if a teacher has segmented it.

syntax: rules governing the ordering of words in a sentence.

systematic instruction: instruction organized in a logical manner to achieve a set of objectives; sequencing may be implied in such an organization but it may depend on a child's progress, so that systematic instruction may not adhere to a rigid sequence.

Tier 2 word: any member of approximately 7,000 word families that is not associated with a particular content subject, that is important to academic success, and that a child will typically not encounter in the course of conversation (e.g., *fortunate, ridiculous*).

valid assessment: a test that adequately addresses the purpose for which it is administered; validity may concern how a construct, skill, or standard is conceptualized and reflected in the test, how well a test predicts a future outcome, or how well it correlates with another measure given at nearly the same time; validity requires that the test be reliable but reliability in itself is not enough to assure validity (cf. **reliable assessment**).

vocabulary: in general, word knowledge; however, the term *vocabulary* is often preceded by a qualifier that limits its scope by function (e.g., meaning vocabulary, sight vocabulary, listening vocabulary).

vowel team: two or more vowel letters appearing together in a word and representing a single vowel sound (also called a vowel combination).

word family: a set of words sharing the same orthographic feature; most commonly, word families consist of rhyming words (e.g., *cat, bat, mat*), but they can also be based on the same onset (e.g., *cat, cab, can*).

word recognition: the composite set of abilities by which a reader associates printed words with their spoken equivalents; these abilities include phoneme–grapheme relationships (phonics), sight words, knowledge of affixes, and recognition of compounds and contractions.

References

Adams, M. J. (1990). *Beginning to read: Thinking and learning about print.* Cambridge, MA: MIT Press.

Adams, M. J., Foorman, B. R., Lundberg, I., & Beeler, T. (1997). *Phonemic awareness in young children: A classroom curriculum.* Baltimore: Brookes.

Anthony, J. L., & Lonigan, C. L. (2004). The nature of phonological awareness: Converging evidence from four studies of preschool and early grade school children. *Journal of Educational Psychology, 96,* 43–55.

Armbruster, B. B., Lehr, F., & Osborn, J. (2001). *Put reading first: The research building blocks for teaching children to read.* Retrieved May 10, 2006, from *www.nifl.gov/partnershipforreading/publications/reading_first1.html.*

Ball, E. W., & Blachman, B. A. (1991). Does phoneme awareness training in kindergarten make a difference in early word recognition and developmental spelling? *Reading Research Quarterly, 26,* 49–66.

Baumann, J. F., & Kame'enui, E. J. (Eds.). (2004). *Vocabulary instruction: Research to practice.* New York: Guilford Press.

Bear, D. R., Invernizzi, M., Templeton, S., & Johnston, F. (2004). *Words their way: Word study for phonics, vocabulary, and spelling instruction* (4th ed.). Upper Saddle River, NJ: Pearson.

Beck, I. L., McKeown, M. G., & Kucan, L. (2002). *Bringing words to life: Robust vocabulary instruction.* New York: Guilford Press.

Biemiller, A., & Slonim, N. (2001). Estimating root word vocabulary growth in normative and advantaged populations: Evidence for a common sequence of vocabulary acquisition. *Journal of Educational Psychology, 93,* 498–520.

Blachman, B. A., Ball, E. W., Black, M. S., & Tangel, D. M. (2000). *Road to the code: A phonological awareness program for young children.* Baltimore: Brookes.

Block, C. C., & Pressley, M. (Eds.). (2002). *Comprehension instruction: Research-based best practices.* New York: Guilford Press.

Boulineau, T., Fore, C., III, Hagan-Burke, S., & Burke, M. D. (2004). Use of story-mapping to increase the story grammar text comprehension of elementary students with learning disabilities. *Learning Disability Quarterly, 27*(2), 105–121.

Brabham, E. G., & Lynch-Brown, C. (2002). Effects of teachers' reading-aloud style on vocabulary acquisition and comprehension of students in the early elementary grades. *Journal of Educational Psychology, 94,* 465–473.

Bursuck, W. D., Smith, T., Munk, D., Damer, M., Mehlig, L., & Perry, J. (2004). Evaluating the impact of a prevention-based model of reading on children who are at risk. *Remedial and Special Education, 25,* 303–313.

Chard, D. J., Vaughn, S., & Tyler, B. J. (2002). A synthesis of research on effective interventions for building reading fluency with elementary students with disabilities. *Journal of Learning Disabilities, 35,* 386–406.

Clark, K. F. (2004). What can I say besides "sound it out"? Coaching word recognition in beginning reading. *Reading Teacher, 57,* 440–449.

Collins, M. F. (2005). ESL preschoolers' English vocabulary acquisition from storybook reading. *Reading Research Quarterly, 40,* 406–408.

Connor, C. M., Morrison, F. J., & Katch, L. E. (2004). Beyond the reading wars: Exploring the effect of child-instruction interactions on growth in early reading. *Scientific Studies of Reading, 8,* 305–336.

Connor, C. M., Morrison, F. J., & Petrella, J. N. (2004). Effective reading comprehension instruction: Examining child × instruction interactions. *Journal of Educational Psychology, 96,* 682–698.

Cunningham, J. W., Spadorcia, S. A., Erickson, K. A., Koppenhaver, D. A., Sturm, J. M., & Yoder, D. E. (2005). Investigating the instructional supportiveness of leveled texts. *Reading Research Quarterly, 40,* 410–427.

Cunningham, P. M. (2005). *Phonics they use: Words for reading and writing.* Upper Saddle River, NJ: Pearson.

Duffy, G. G. (2003). *Explaining reading: A resource for teaching concepts, skills, and strategies.* New York: Guilford Press.

Ehri, L. (1997). Sight word learning in normal readers and dyslexics. In B. Blachman (Ed.), *Foundations of reading acquisition and dyslexia: Implications for early intervention* (pp. 163–189). Mahwah, NJ: Erlbaum.

Ericson, L., & Juliebö, M. F. (1998). *The phonological awareness handbook for kindergarten and primary teachers.* Newark, DE: International Reading Association.

Eskey, D. E. (2002). Reading and the teaching of L2 reading. *TESOL Journal, 11,* 5–9.

Fountas, I. C., & Pinnell, G. S. (1996). *Guided reading: Good first teaching for all children.* Portsmouth, NH: Heinemann.

Fox, B. J. (2005). *Phonics for the teacher of reading.* Upper Saddle River, NJ: Pearson.

Fry, E. (1980). The new instant word list. *Reading Teacher, 34,* 284–289.

Fry, E. (2004). Phonics: A large phoneme-grapheme frequency count revised. *Journal of Literacy Research, 36,* 85–98.

Ganske, K. (2000) *Word journeys: Assessment-guided phonics, spelling, and vocabulary instruction.* New York: Guilford Press.

Gaskins, I. W. (1999). Problem solving: Struggling readers. *Reading Teacher, 53,* 162–164.

Gaskins, I. W. (2005). *Success with struggling readers: The Benchmark School approach.* New York: Guilford Press.

Gaskins, I., Ehri, L., & Cress, C. (1996). Procedures for word learning: Making discoveries about words. *Reading Teacher, 50,* 312–327.

Gillet, J. W., & Kita, M. J. (1979). Words, kids, and categories. *Reading Teacher, 32,* 538–546.

Graves, M. F. (1986). Vocabulary learning and instruction, In E. Z. Rothkopf (Ed.), *Review of research in education* (Vol. 13, pp. 49–91). Washington, DC: American Educational Research Association.

Guthrie, J. T., Wigfield, A., Barbosa, P., Perencevich, K. C., Taboada, A., Davis, M. H., et al. (2004). Increasing reading comprehension and engagement through Concept-Oriented Reading Instruction. *Journal of Educational Psychology, 96,* 403–423.

Hare, V. C., & Borchardt, K. M. (1984). Direct instruction of summarization skills. *Reading Research Quarterly, 20,* 62–78.

Hart, B., & Risley, T. R. (1995). *Meaningful differences in the everyday experience of young American children.* Baltimore: Brookes.

Hasbrouck, J., & Tindal, G. A. (2006). Oral reading fluency norms: A valuable assessment tool for reading teachers. *Reading Teacher, 59,* 636–644.

Heibert, E. H., & Martin, L. A. (2002). The texts of beginning reading instruction. In S. B. Neuman & D. K. Dickinson (Eds.), *Handbook of early literacy research* (pp. 361–376). New York: Guilford Press.

Hickman, P., Pollard-Durodola, S., & Vaughn, S. (2004). Storybook reading: Improving vocabulary and comprehension for English-language learners. *Reading Teacher, 57,* 720–730.

Hollingsworth, P. M. (1978). An experimental approach to the impress method of teaching reading. *Reading Teacher, 31,* 624–626.

Hudson, R. F., Lane, H. C., & Pullen, P. C. (2005). Reading fluency assessment and instruction: What, why, and how? *Reading Teacher, 58,* 702–714.

Invernizzi, M., Rosemary, C., Juel, C., & Richards, H. C. (1997). At-risk readers and community volunteers: A 3–year perspective. *Scientific Studies of Reading, 1,* 277–300.

Jitendra, A. K., Edwards, L. L., Sacks, G., & Jacobson, L. A. (2004). What research says about vocabulary instruction for students with learning disabilities. *Exceptional Children, 70,* 299–322.

Johnson, D. D., & Pearson, P. D. (1984). *Teaching reading vocabulary* (2nd ed.). New York: Holt, Rinehart & Winston.

Juel, C. (1988). Learning to read and write: A longitudinal study of fifty-four children from first through fourth grade. *Journal of Educational Psychology, 80,* 437–447.

Justice, L. M., Meier, J., & Walpole, S. (2005). Learning new words from storybooks: An efficacy study for at-risk kindergarteners. *Journal of Speech, Language, and Hearing Services in the Schools, 36,* 17–32.

Kim, A. H., Vaughn, S., Wanzek, J., & Wei, S. (2004). Graphic organizers and their effects on the reading comprehension of students with LD: A synthesis of research. *Journal of Learning Disabilities, 37,* 105–118.

Kintsch, E. (2005). Comprehension theory as a guide for the design of thoughtful questions. *Topics in Language Disorders, 25,* 51–64.

Kuhn, M. (2004). Helping students become accurate, expressive readers: Fluency instruction for small groups. *Reading Teacher, 58,* 338–344.

Kuhn, M. R., & Stahl, S. A. (2003). Fluency: A review of developmental and remedial practices. *Journal of Educational Psychology, 95,* 3–21.

Marzano, R. J. (2004). The developing vision of vocabulary instruction. In J. F. Baumann & E. G. Kame'enui (Eds.), *Vocabulary instruction: Research to practice* (pp. 100–117). New York: Guilford Press.

Mathes, P., Denton, C., & Fletcher, J. (2005). The effects of theoretically different instruction and student characteristics on the skills of struggling readers. *Reading Research Quarterly, 40,* 148–182.

McGee, L. M., & Morrow, L. M. (2005). *Teaching literacy in kindergarten.* New York: Guilford Press.

McKenna, M. C., & Stahl, S. A. (2003). *Assessment for reading instruction.* New York: Guilford Press.

McKenna, M. C., & Walpole, S. (2005). How well does assessment inform our reading instruction? *Reading Teacher, 59,* 84–86.

Menon, S., & Hiebert, E. H. (2005). A comparison of first graders' reading with little books or literature-based basal anthologies. *Reading Research Quarterly, 40,* 12–38.

Moats, L. C. (2000). *Speech to print: Language essentials for teachers.* Baltimore: Brookes.

Morris, D., Shaw, B., & Perney, J. (1990). Helping low readers in grades 2 and 3: An after-school volunteer tutorial program. *Elementary School Journal, 9,* 133–150.

National Institute for Literacy. (n.d.). *Put reading first: Helping your child learn to read.* Retrieved May 10, 2006, from *www.nifl.gov/partnershipforreading/publications/Parent_br.pdf.*

National Institute of Child Health and Human Development. (2000). *Report of the National Reading Panel: Teaching children to read—an evidence-based assessment of the scientific research literature on reading and its implications for reading instruction* (NIH Publication No. 00–4769). Washington, DC: U.S. Government Printing Office.

Oudeans, M. K. (2003). Integration of letter–sound correspondences and phonological awareness skills of blending and segmenting: A pilot study examining the effects of instructional sequence on word reading for kindergarten children with low phonological awareness. *Learning Disability Quarterly, 26(4),* 258–280.

Pearson, P. D., & Gallagher, M. C. (1983). The instruction of reading comprehension. *Contemporary Educational Psychology, 8,* 317–344.

Pearson, P. D., & Johnson, D. D. (1978). *Teaching reading comprehension.* New York: Holt, Rinehart & Winston.

Pikulski, J. J., & Chard, D. J. (2005). Fluency: Bridge between decoding and reading comprehension. *Reading Teacher, 58,* 510–519.

Pittelman, S. D., Heimlich, J. E., Berglund, R. L., & French, M. P. (1991). *Semantic feature analysis: Classroom applications.* Newark, DE: International Reading Association.

Pressley, M. (2006). *Reading instruction that works: The case for balanced teaching* (3rd ed.). New York: Guilford Press.

RAND Reading Study Group. (2002). *Reading for understanding: Toward an R&D program in reading comprehension.* Santa Monica, CA: RAND.

Raphael, T. E. (1986). Teaching question–answer relationships, revisited. *Reading Teacher, 39,* 516–523.

Rasinski, T. V. (2003). *The fluent reader: Oral reading strategies for building word recognition, fluency, and comprehension.* New York: Scholastic Professional Books.

Rasinski, T. V., Padak, N., Linek, W., & Sturtevant, E. (1994). The effects of fluency development instruction on urban second grade readers. *Journal of Educational Research, 87,* 158–164.

Rasinski, T. V., & Zimmerman, B. S. (2001). *Phonics poetry: Teaching word families.* Boston: Allyn & Bacon.

Reutzel, D. R., Smith, J. A., & Fawson, P. C. (2005). An evaluation of two approaches for teaching reading comprehension strategies in the primary years using science information text. *Early Childhood Research Quarterly, 20,* 276–305.

Roberts, T. (2003). Effects of alphabet-letter instruction on young children's word recognition. *Journal of Educational Psychology, 95,* 41–51.

Samuels, S. J. (1979). The method of repeated readings. *Reading Teacher, 32,* 241–254.

Santi, K. L., Menchetti, B. M., & Edwards, B. J. (2004). A comparison of eight kindergarten phonemic awareness programs based on empirically validated instructional principles. *Remedial and Special Education, 25,* 189–196.

Schwartz, R. M., & Raphael, T. E. (1985). Concept of definition: A key to improving students' vocabulary. *Reading Teacher, 39,* 198–205.

Simmons, D. C., & Kame'enui, E. J. (1999). Curriculum maps: Mapping instruction to achieve instructional priorities in beginning reading, kindergarten–grade 3. Retrieved May 2, 2006, from *http://reading.uoregon.edu/appendices.maps.php.*

Stafford, K. B., Williams, J. P., Nubla-Kung, A., & Pollini, S. (2005). Teaching at-risk second graders text structure via social studies content. *Teaching Exceptional Children, 38(2),* 62–65.

Stahl, S. A., & Heubach, K. M. (2005). Fluency-oriented reading instruction. *Journal of Literacy Research, 37,* 25–60.

Stahl, S. A., & Nagy, W. E. (2005). *Teaching word meanings.* Mahwah, NJ: Erlbaum.

Sweet, A. P., & Snow, C. E. (Eds.). (2003). *Rethinking reading comprehension.* New York: Guilford Press.

Taba, H. (1967). *Teacher's handbook for elementary social studies.* Reading, MA: Addison-Wesley.

Therrien, W. J. (2004). Fluency and comprehension gains as a result of repeated reading. *Remedial and Special Education, 25,* 252–261.

Tolman, C. (2005). Working smarter, not harder: What teachers of reading need to know and be able to teach. *Perspectives, 31(4),* 15–23.

Tomlinson, C. A. (1999). *The differentiated classroom: Responding to the needs of all learners.* Alexandria, VA: Association for Supervision and Curriculum Development.

Trabasso, T., van den Broek, P., & Lui, L. (1988). A model for generating questions that assess and promote comprehension. *Questioning Exchange, 2,* 25–38.

Walpole, S., & McKenna, M. C. (2004). *The literacy coach's handbook: A guide to research-based practice.* New York: Guilford Press.

White, T. G. (2005). Effects of systematic and strategic analogy-based phonics on grade 2 students' word reading and reading comprehension. *Reading Research Quarterly, 40,* 234–255.

Williams, C., & Hufnagel, K. (2005). The impact of word study instruction on kindergarten children's journal writing. *Research in the Teaching of English, 39,* 233–270.

Williams, J. P. (2005). Instruction in reading comprehension for primary-grade students: A focus on text structure. *Journal of Special Education, 39,* 6–18.

Wylie, R. E., & Durrell, D. D. (1970). Teaching vowels through phonograms. *Elementary English, 47,* 787–791.

Index

Entries with bold page numbers refer to glossary terms;
"f" following a page number represents a figure.